A DUBIOUS JOURNEY

From Class to Class

By Anne Near

Hereford Publishing Company

Copyright © 1993 Hereford Publishing

Grateful acknowledgement to:

Project Director - Holly Near
Manuscript & Design Editor - Mary K. Bugnon
Production Advisor - Jo-Lynne Worley
Technical Editor - Jan Jue

Library of Congress Cataloging-in-Publication Data

CIP 92-076050

Near, Anne
    A DUBIOUS JOURNEY From Class to Class : an autobiography / Anne Near
        p.   cm.

ISBN 0-9635674-0-3

Printed in the United States of America.

Cover drawing done by Dorothy Smith Holmes.

CONTENTS

ACKNOWLEDGEMENTS

To Russell, who expressed no apprehension whatsoever when I spent whole days at my typewriter, and to our four children, Timothy, Holly, Fred and Laurel, whose adult lives are not a whit like mine.

And remembering, one by one, the unique contribution of each person, I acknowledge my heartfelt gratitude to Jo-Lynne Worley, Jan Jue, Dorothy Andersen, Annette Parks, Barbara Saul Jacobson, Anne Rothschild, Martha Blagden, Catherine Coulson, Jean Hinton, Erika Makino, Sunlight, Margene McGee, Pam Levin, Krissy Keefer and Rain Burns. The order in which they are named is without significance; my thanks is luminously specific.

Finally, my thanks to Holly Near and Mary K. Bugnon, for seeing this project through to completion.

INTRODUCTION
By Holly Near

This project started out as an article Mom agreed to do for a friend of hers, Dorothy Andersen, who was writing a book about *downward mobility* - people who had been born with money and who chose lifestyles which took them down into the so-called lower classes. The work got Mom thinking about her past and the article initiated what has become an elaborate journal...a journal in the tradition of womens' writings, women sitting in their rooms behind typewriters, or with pen in hand, in the wee hours of the night, after the children and husbands and household responsibilities are tucked away. For most of my life I can remember the sound of Mom's typewriter.

Anne's story, mostly unedited and so completely her, is a mix of radical contemporary 90's thought and poetic Victorian language. Sometimes she uses unfamiliar sentence structures and mysterious words, sending me off to the dictionary to discover her meaning and leaving me in a state of wonder. Why don't I know these words? Has the era of television robbed us of language and poetry and the patience to linger in the detail of description? I envy her vast vocabulary and her ability to use it.

In the commercial or patriarchal sense, this is neither a history book nor a documented investigation. But in the tradition of remembering, it is, as Anne says, "...a multidimensional blend of landscape, portraiture, film clip...familiar but not exactly as one sees oneself reflected in a store window, a bunch of dates scrawled illegibly on a United Nations Children's Calendar..."

Although Mom insists on calling it a "dubious journey", from the point of view of this daughter, it was not dubious at all. It required an extraordinary amount of courage, in a pre-feminist era, to take the steps that this woman took to say goodbye to wealth and all that it meant then, both practically and symbolically, in America.

I encourage all of us to get our parents to talk, to write, to remember, to leave us the stories. We are so dependent now on telephone calls and so drawn to television that not only is the art of story telling lost, so are the stories. This is a beautiful gift Anne has given to her children, so that when our children ask, "Who was my grandmother? Who was my grandfather? Who was Kate? Who was Ruth? What was it like in those days?", we will have something to tell them - something personal, poetic and political.

But my friends assure me this book extends beyond the family. It recounts a piece of the past that we have almost lost and weaves it to our present, as we struggle so hard to comprehend our future.

for Ruth

Woodcut made by Ruth Holmes, for
our mother, as a bookplate (her hat,
gardening gloves and trowel), 1934.

PREFACE

The journey I proclaim is the one to be taken from class to class - some might say *downward*. It would never have occurred to me to describe my life in these terms were it not for Dorothy Andersen, a Quaker, and a conversation she had with a friend. The subject was *upward mobility*, words viable at the time. Her friend had joked, "I guess I'm *downwardly mobile!*" Dorothy had observed this trend among her acquaintances. She elicited essays to the point, and then came out with a book, *Reaching New Heights Through Downward Mobility* - to say the least, a partisan title.

The language *downward mobility* floats upstream against the dreams of a nation of immigrants. It offends our inculcated shape of mind. North American literature is rich in testimonial stories about parents who worked sacrificially so that their children could go to college, or in some other way qualify for lives that would not be dragged down by laboring for someone better off; so that their offspring or they themselves could be that more affluent person. Without denigrating the intergenerationally generous and spiritual aspects of those hopes, I recognize that educational goals have been dominated less by the hunger for wisdom than by the goal of economic access and an upward change of class. Not so for me.

This is not to forget that bare survival was the primary struggle - often lost - for thousands who came to this land in chains, or fled persecution, or challenged the invincibility of poverty that was, at that time, considered preordained by birth. Nor do I presume to plumb the pre-invasion consciousness of the aboriginals on the continent recently named American, whose cultures expressed an awesome comfort within creation, but one can infer that, although they had their own territorial wars, upward mobility was not their abiding concern. And then let's not overlook that a system offering basic needs - shelter, food, health and child care - would have rendered a different poll on human priorities. I wonder what choices would people make in their life journey if offended dignity and an empty stomach were not their inspirations - or as in my case, the escape from the embarrassment of wealth and privilege. Who would we all be if money were not the major definer!

However, there was a powerful and dominating obsession that drove many Europeans to the deadly war of trying to "get ahead." They did not worry much about depleting the apparently endless resources "discovered in the New World." The idea of frugality was a moral one, deriving not so much from an awareness of planetary finitude as from the rigors of pioneer life or fear of envy for having more than others. Some had no qualms about committing genocide, ridding themselves of the inconvenience of people who got in their way. They had no conflict with using long hours of female, child, and imported labor, for they could not have completed this westward expansion without them. And as they succeeded in dominating all forms of life, horrendous dumpsites began to attest to the fact that the disapproval of waste, learned in their own brush with poverty did not modify their behavior appreciably. Having the habit of taking all that was wanted from Mother Earth, the Nordic descendants had to find their way to the moon and then look back before they could comprehend what the people erroneously called "Indians" had warned all along. *Take only what you need and use all you take!* There are revolutionary questions. How much does one need? How much do others need? Unconsciously I must have begun to revise the presumptions of my lifestyle when in search of the answer to this one.

When I was invited - because of my known junket across life's choices - to share my experiences of *downward mobility*, I came across an article by Rita Mae Brown. It was entitled "The Last Straw," and was excerpted from her book *Plain Brown Wrapper*. In it the author addresses the concept of *downward mobility*, calling it the greatest insult yet derived by middle class people against the working class. She acknowledges that for some middle class women, *downward mobility* had been a first attempt to start changing their ways that were hurtful to others, but she found the attempt "fatally flawed exactly because these women could afford to reject materialism."

If you have money, Sister, don't deny it, share it. If you have advanced skills, don't make pottery in your loft, teach us your skills. If you have good clothes, don't walk around in rags, give us some of your clothes. *Downward mobility* is a way to deny your material privileges to prove how "right on" you are. We know that any time you get tired of poverty you can go right back to them.

With this fortuitous warning - once again, books find me out - I begin my story.

CHAPTER ONE

My Parents' Ways

As long as I can remember, I wanted to be *downwardly mobile*, although I had never run into those particular words; they were not on every billboard seventy-four years ago. I did not want to live on a hill with a commanding view, but rather to stand in a fertile valley and be proud in a working relationship with dirt, mud, soil, earth and rain falling on it and the people tilling it. When I was driven, with my parents, through the countryside of Brittany in a chauffeured limousine, with our steamer trunks, golf clubs, tennis rackets and beach chairs strapped on the roof, I would shyly glance with profound wistfulness at the peasants in the fields who stopped their work to stare at rich Americans in flight. Our native driver wore his uniform, a white duster, dark glasses, a little visor cap; no one would mistake him for us. He sped through the narrow streets without sidewalks, blowing his outrageous horn. Who was he! Did he really think we were so important that chickens should scurry out of the way? Was he deriding us, displaying his catch, so that he could return to his people with some of the wealth we scattered around? Mortified, Ruth and I sometimes hid below the window as the charming towns we had come to see were left behind - Lucy le Bocage, Les Andelys, Honfleur.

   When we stopped for the night, my father would ask for the best rooms in the hotel; my mother loved a balcony with a view, and my father felt insulted if he was offered less than all. My mother used her Baedeker to guide us to the loveliest, history-laden places. *Quimper! Rouen of Renan and Joan of Arc! St. Jean de Luz! Carcassonne!* I cannot fault my mother's taste. Our luggage would arrive in our ample quarters. My mother would rush to

1

scrub the already gleaming bathroom facilities. This was the only time she performed these chores, but she knew how. She did not want us catching diseases. Whose diseases? Foreign people's? The good folks of Normandy? I never asked and never helped. I was young. I did not worry about diseases in 1929.

When the rituals had been accomplished, my sister and I would escape while my mother rested and my father touched base with "the people"...on the tennis courts or golf course. Ruth and I would seek out some semblance of contact through the cobbled streets and little stores - perhaps find a china figurine to bring home, or a pastry shop where we could try out the language with someone real. Our adventures were limited by who we appeared to be, and in fact were: sheltered girl children of Americans; we received courteous attention, which we tried to deserve by sensitive behavior. This was in a time before the seemingly endless years when the United States government would sorely tax the natural affection of our motherlands. At that time, people seemed to have an unqualified liking for Americans, and we tried to behave in harmony with that blessing by disassociating ourselves from a hurtful display of wealth.

Especially while traveling, I became aware of a duality that had been trying to define itself in me, as if I were not leading my own life. Only temporarily was I enjoying my parents' world; my own had already started elsewhere in the arms of a working-class Irish nanny.

However, I traveled through my parents' ways in the manner that Americans journeyed abroad - even to the moon - the better to see themselves against many backdrops, and I enjoyed their homes immensely. My first domestic memory is of a two-story white country house in Noroton, Connecticut. The shades are pulled down because my brother has just hit my sister in the eye with a golf ball. He is coming in for some pretty heavy criticism, as usual, along with the general dismay. But I know it was not his intended fault; his aim is not that accurate! I sympathize with him, the accused. I still sympathize with the accused. Lawrance gave me many opportunities to practice empathy.

Then I remember a house on Manhattan near Lexington Avenue; five houses lined the north side of the block, five houses

2

lined the south side, with an extraordinary garden in the center shared by all. I wonder if our house still has the food elevator that raised the meals from the kitchen to the dining level. My memories become slightly more significant after the family moved to an apartment three stories above the street. The whole floor was ours. There were large windows from which we could lean out and toss pennies to the costumed ragamuffins who roamed the streets on Halloween. It was clear to me, those kids had the best of it; this could not be verified because we were never allowed to walk their neighborhood.

Our Park Avenue flat was spacious. With roller skates - two-wheelers! - Central Park was our backyard. One Pekingese was the only animal to live with us here; a boy from the Third Avenue tenements was paid ten cents a day to take him for a fastidious walk in the gutters of Seventy-second Street. For our exercise, a bar was installed across our hall so that we could go with a swing and stretch our backs. A full-sized pool table easily found room in the foyer. There was a study with many books and large, overstuffed chairs. The parlor entertained a grand piano; here, too, was enshrined a mind-boggling innovation, a record changer, one of the first, that could provide continuous, hand-chosen music. It shuffled a stack of brittle discs with classical red and gold labels - often disastrously.

I so easily refer to "we" or "us" as if I were saying "I." It is appropriate for one who has lived life as an identical twin; I had the joyous privilege and peculiar security of a constant companion my own exact age. Ruth! A few paragraphs back I spoke her name without even stopping to introduce her. This given, a relationship neither solicited nor won, also had the disadvantage of a self-actualizing mirror ever in my view. It doubled the shame, as it were, as well as the rapture. We suffered equally when she or I did something wrong. In our seventy-fifth year, she reminds me that she hated herself when I broke someone's front permanent tooth while playing at a drinking fountain! We were part of each other.

My brother had a room of his own when he was not shipped off to boarding school in Aiken, South Carolina - a burden laid on him since he was ten because he had contracted rheumatic fever after being taken with his class, in the cold of a New York winter, to an apartment house rooftop to watch an eclipse of the moon. He was also sent to *prep school* to be groomed to take his place among future leaders of men. If I had known the words at the time, I would have figured this would take considerable *upward mobility* on his part. We wept with him when he was trundled off in his gray flannel shorts, jacket and little cap, to grow up in the care of British masters. We loved Lawrance, Ruth and I. Only he could divide our twinship; we would betray each other for his favor. While he was away, his room became the province of a woman who "did the sewing." I cannot imagine what this sewing was, for my mother had clothes sent home from Saks Fifth Avenue and Bonwit Teller and expensive little shops opened by two of her friends whose husbands' wealth-making faltered during the Depression. My father's suits were tailored by Brooks Brothers. Notwithstanding, Mrs. Hubner stitched away, her knuckles gnarled by arthritis, her environment littered with pins.

My parents' room had windows on both Park Avenue and Seventy-Second Street. They retired here from five-thirty until the cocktail hour at eight. Beyond the living room, scene of this moderate but unfailing alcoholism, waited a well-appointed dining room, a pantry, a kitchen and, on a smaller scale than ours, rooms (never to be invaded by us kids, but never afforded the privacy of locks) for the exclusive use of the help - a butler, a parlor maid, a cook, a kitchen maid and a lady who took care of my mother's wardrobe. A certain national hierarchy was to be sensed in this cast. The butler was English usually, although one was Norwegian; I think Nils lost his job by winking at us. Did I tell? I can't remember, but I know the cook was Swedish because "Swedes made the best biscuits." The maids were French or Scandinavian; all nurses Scottish or Irish. The Middle European countries were never represented, nor were people of Jewish or African descent; presumably they would not be happy east of Central Park or south of Harlem. Our governesses were English with hopefully contagious accents, or French, with the charge of teaching us the most appropriate foreign language; we resisted mightily and effectively. To borrow from a beloved television drama, governesses belonged neither "upstairs" nor "downstairs." To me, the women who played this role were politely tolerated, barely; I loved no one of them. Do others take this role today in

4

the ménage of the rich? I do not know, being excluded from such information by my *downward mobility*.

All of these characters - I chose no way to relate to them otherwise, lest by familiarity I embarrass all of us - accompanied our family to a summer home in Old Brookville, Long Island, where their accommodations were sunnier than in the city but in the same size ratio...much smaller. They were not invited to play tennis on our court or use the swimming pool or go to the Piping Rock Country Club where these amenities were duplicated in attractive ways that included the shores of Long Island Sound. Our grounds were tended by a German gardener and a Swedish second-man. Their wives did the winter caretaking of the summer house, the fruit canning and jam making and the laundry. Albert and Vera Rother had a son called Frankie who grew up to be an employee of Kodak in Rochester, New York; Pietr and Hulde had a fat little son called Pintee, and he, too, may have become upwardly mobile, hopefully to his pleasure.

There were horses supposedly taken care of by my sister and me, but in retrospect this seems unrealistic. We did well with them when it was the season for jumping these elegant hunters over rail fences, or hitching a little Welsh pony to a tippy go-cart with two tall wheels and driving fast along the lanes of the large estates; for the rest of the year, someone else was bringing them in and out of the classic red barn and feeding them hay with a rasher of grain. Expensive toys! Playing with Flash and Bobbie Shot and Queenie proved to be of unexpected value when horses carried me to elucidating experiences of poverty with dignity in the Appalachian Mountains, USA, where I, as a volunteer, rode out with the midwives of the Frontier Nursing Service.

My parents entertained a lot, hosting or going out for dinner many days of each week. Delicious meals were served on time, by contract between those who knew how to prepare the best and those who expected it. Since I'm no longer wealthy, I can't observe the lifestyle of young rich families today, but I imagine a wholly different timing incompatible with yesteryear - more spontaneous, less commitment to pattern, but, of course, still with a lot of "help," unavailable to the middle- and working-class families around me today. My parents dressed for dinner; they put the day away. When we children were too young to wait up

5

for a formal meal, we were served early, requiring double cooking or rather, triple cooking, for the staff had its own menu. I can envisage my mother, still in bed with a silky coverlet, still resting while the cook stood bedside, pad in hand. Together they would plan the repasts, complicated by the multiple preparations. "The servants" preferred an early dinner. If they had eaten after us, they could have carved from the family roast, but then that would have them eating at nine o'clock. However, we could not be presented with a half-sampled dish if they ate first, so two, and sometimes three, complete (and no doubt, different) menus...the servants, the children, the adults. Occasionally, the children were allowed to stand politely at a parent's side to sample the epicurean creations being passed. It was our chance to learn. "Taste?"

Our closets and bureaus were always filled with freshly laundered clothes, sweet-smelling, starched and ironed in a time before permanent press. Mostly, we wore dark-green serge uniforms - light-green cotton in the spring - because our excellent institution of learning did not want apparel rivalry between the daughters of the rich and a little less rich. We were all girls at Miss Chapin's School, kindergarten through twelfth grade. Even in this select setting, my mother had Mrs. Hubner sew our blouses with round rather than pointed collars. I wish I had pressed her to explain why. During the Depression, as today, uniforms saved a lot of face.

I am surprised to notice that I have mentioned Chapin here for the first time and in a rather frivolous context. Perhaps the school was so much a part of my world that it is as invisible in my memory as the fresh air we used to breathe without a sigh; I was chauffeur-delivered to its door for thirteen years. If my childhood and adolescence had a standard complement of sorrow and confusion, Chapin provided a grounding I now perceive as enviable. The school's almost absolute degree of exclusivity, produced a milieu in which prejudice had no cause to flower; there was no reason to develop this lamentable vice; there was no black girl to invite me to a home in Harlem, no Jewish girl for me to visit on the West Side, no Puerto Rican to study Latin with; there was no Spanish language taught in our school. There was no one to leave out or to leave me out.

6

The twins moved through Chapin on a slow wave of popularity engendered by their amusing dual-identity. We answered to each other's names, knowing that it was only our names that our friends mixed up. We knew which was which, and so did they. We never played at fooling people - never. When, in my senior year I failed to pass a College Board exam and, by school law, could not then assume the elective office of school president, the loyal administration allowed Ruth and me to change places: she became president and I, vice-sident and I, vice-president. Who cared! It hardly rippled the waters.

One year I broke my arm high-jumping in the wet spring grass. It was set by one of New York's noted surgeons who happened to be playing golf with my father that Sunday. Even with a much-autographed plaster cast, I managed to dislodge Dr. Eugene Poole's impromptu masterpiece; now with the bones staunchly sealed out of kilter, my injury merited the attention of this top-notch craftsman! My team shifted players so that I could be the one-arm goalie when we played field hockey on lush grass that Chapin maintained, a nice train ride up the Hudson River shore. The green and the gold! We wore yellow or green tunics; our teams played only each other.

In the infrastructure that used to be referred to as high society, parents seemed to think they had to keep boys and girls apart to do their learning - that is, book learning. Why else would they send their dearest boy children away to boarding school to be taught by British masters in an Anglican setting, and their girls to private schools at home? Our parents did, however, buy into a very beautiful way for us to get a glimpse of each other, the boys sweating in their tuxedos like sweet, nervous penguins, and the girls shivering in low-back, low-front evening gowns like child queens, waltzing together under the sparkling cut-glass chandeliers of the Plaza Hotel ballroom.

All the prep school boys wanted a bid to The Ball. Each girl was allowed to bring two boys. My brother had a big chip in his pocket; with twin sisters, he could do four boys a favor. Still, he criticized, "Why don't you talk?" I implored, "What about, Lorry? I can't think of a thing to say to your friends." "Talk about nothing! Learn to talk about nothing! That's what Julie does." Lawrance had a girlfriend. Girls had the power of invitation, but the power ended when they stepped out on the ballroom floor. It was an unspoken rule and a matter of politesse that one of the two escorts must dance the first dance with the one who invited him, to get her started. After that, it was open season, too slow or too fast or just right. If she did not appear "popular," even a friend would hesitate to "cut in," for fear of being "stuck." It was embarrassing to notice boys signaling in barely veiled desperation. "Come on, guys, cut in on me! I promise on a stack of Bibles, I'll get some other guy to cut in on you. I swear it!" That's how it worked. There was no acceptable way for a couple to separate except by being "cut in on."

At the Plaza Hotel, the boys huddled in the center of the ballroom, gazing, strategizing, circled by the braver dancing couples. They would soon become doctors, lawyers, merchants, thieves, stockbrokers, ambassadors, generals or presidents, but for the moment, their formation was called "the stag line." Some boys never ventured out to ask a girl to dance, lest they find themselves dancing with a virtual stranger all evening. But many were brave and made the most of an enchanting *mise-en-scène*. It was Mrs. Hubbard, the dancing teacher - apparently, the only acceptable one - who yearly choreographed these holiday events. The waltz was the poem of her life; all fall she taught the girls how to "follow" even the boys' most inept body signals, except in this, that they teach the boys the difference between a waltz and a fox-trot. One, two, three, step, two, three, turn, two, three, dip, two, three! She had been known even to corral a boy and make him get it right - thus way exceeding the boundaries of her class.

I dance my very best. I follow my partner's lead. I owe it to him to look as if I'm having a lovely time. I act out fun. I am not stuck yet! The most popular girls never get to really dance with anyone for more than a few steps. My best friend is one of these; the boy she brought feels cheated by her popularity - someone is always cutting in. I try to sympathize and pray he won't be stuck with me. Then - in the stag line - I see Augie. I am overjoyed. He is not Adonis, not yet. He takes a slide across the floor. I feel his hand touch the shoulder of my partner who had sunk into a whirlpool of silence and rhythm. I hear Augie's polite request for permission to cut in, a permission that cannot be refused. He dances to the side of the ballroom floor, and then leads me to a table surrounded by spindly chairs with red velvet cushions. We actually listen to the music of Eddie Duchin. A waiter puts scrambled eggs in front of us. Augie acts enraptured, as if he rarely got to eat at all. And then he talks. His eloquence makes a listener out of me. Someday, he would write an engaging book, The Public Happiness, and I would write about cattle ranching where the protagonist is an Indian cowboy, veteran to a war that hadn't happened yet when Augie and I danced in the Plaza Hotel ballroom.

The remembrance of August Hecksher persuaded me to give this episode a happy ending; with him it always was. However, the pattern designed for introducing teenage boys and girls to each other was not auspicious. The rites of passage were well-meaning, costly, exquisitely designed, and frequently bright with hidden anguish. How many a young woman, myself included, had to suffer throughout her twenties to finally discover that she could, indeed, be an enjoyable companion to a man. I felt enormous culpability for my unpopularity with men, as measured by the Junior Ball scenario, contributing to the flight factors in my *downward mobility.*

Strolling through my recollections, I find two memories way back before Chapin School moved uptown to the building on the East River, where it now is. When we were at Fifty-seventh Street, our teachers were always imploring us to keep our voices down; truly, the play-screams of some 100 little girls must have been quite excruciating to the ears of metropolitan businessmen with the world to carry on their shoulders. They might even have paid the school to move away, but really, what did they have to worry about in 1922? War was over forever, it had become so awful. Prosperity was here to stay!

My second memory is a more graphic reminder of how long ago this was; horses were still being used to pull delivery wagons through the streets, alongside with cars. One such noble animal had fallen on icy pavement; his feet had then been run over. We are looking down from a height of three stories. Blood gushes. The teacher rushes the children away from the window.

In recounting little glimpses randomly, as oldsters do, while trying to lay hand on childhood - New York City in winter, when our golf stockings still came only to below the knee; spring, delirious after such total withholding of green; Long Island in summer, when our place was sweet with the flowers of locust

9

trees, apples, and pears; autumn when our estate was surrounded by the aromatic fields of purple cabbages tended by Polish women whose names we never thought to ask - I do not mean to imply that this was all we had! As a reprieve from businessman's worry, my father repaired to a rustic camp on Lake Honnedaga, blue and fathoms deep, in the Adirondack Mountains - preserved and, of course, reserved. (I didn't know to call this a Gentile lake, but I learned later that it was and that there were also "Jewish lakes" and "Communist lakes.") All I grasped was that we could all relax without the domestic retinue, although my parents used the help of the rugged guides. These men, who bore no trace of servitude, carried provisions in huge wicker pack baskets shaped to their shoulders, wore magnificently shapeless hats adorned with a *parmecheeni belle* or black hatter fly hook, rowed the boats with silent oars, identified the best fishing holes, cleaned the trout for frying in the large iron pans spitting on the stove with a smokey hiss. When in the Adirondacks, my father adopted their contours, style of hat, and skills. Refreshed, he returned to his gray or pin-striped suits.

Once a summer, an Indian appeared by canoe at our dock. We watched him coming from afar. I am now ashamed that I cannot identify his tribal affiliation, Iroquois or Mohawk. We waited for him. He laid out trinkets now made for sale by people who had thought this land had been given to their use - not "ownership" - by the Great Spirit. I thought so, too. Now, as I write, the spruce trees which gave the skyline a cathedral grandeur have withered under the airborne onslaught of polluting particulates from beyond the mountains. Because I am not usually a creative dreamer - that is, I do not remember my dreams the way my daughter Timothy does, regaling us with stories of her hilarious nocturnal life - I was deeply grateful for one dream vouchsafed me against this backdrop. I rise at dawn and go down to where lake waves gently lap the shore. A tall Indian stands there. He tells me, "Bend down and drink of this water; then you will know all you ever need to know." I felt that way about the Adirondack lake, so deep and clear that one could see a leaf twenty feet down, resting on silt that had not been disturbed for centuries. Ruth's children's children - and Lawrance's too - still go there to drink. Although they may appear to spend most of their time trying to start motorboats, I am not fooled.

My Niece, Toni Famulari, sketched the Adirondack "guides".

CHAPTER TWO

The Homes of Childhood

Quite distinct from school with its scholastic, social, and athletic rituals to which I was wholly dedicated during the academic year, Ruth and I were fortunate in enjoying a quadruplet friendship with Betty Grace and Martha Allen, two girls I considered the most beautiful in the world. Granted, mine was a narrow assessment because both were Caucasian, just my age, and in my class at Miss Chapin's - but school was not the locale of our bond. In the summer, we all lived on Long Island. Our house was an old farmhouse my mother had restored with loving attention to details of colonial authenticity. Betty's was a mansion in the old English mode, with dark wood, white plaster walls, and long red-carpeted halls leading past countless bedroom doors. High tea was prepared with a silver service, delicate china cups, and saucers to balance artfully. Well-bred setters lounged near Russell Grace's hand, never appearing to notice the tiny bite-size sandwiches and cakes.

We were also invited to dine on damask-covered long, long tables eliciting our best behavior; a dime was offered to any child who could manage the many course dishes passed by butlers and plates removed by maids, and not spill a drop on the gleaming white cloth. The moment of verification must have been mortifying, but actually I don't remember it - or that many dimes were awarded. It was not meant to be a financial challenge...Russell and Elise Grace were very generous with their daughters' friends. We played tennis on their indoor court and swam in an outdoor pool reached through grassy walking lanes marked off by hedgerows. Sometimes we four good friends traveled to the Graces' home in Aiken, South Carolina, by train from Manhattan's icy streets right into warm spring, yellow with forsythia. We slept in a large room, light and airy, with four beds, and were brought breakfast on four powder-blue trays with little folding legs, and rode quiet polo ponies along piney trails, never at a gallop, never with abandon.

In these and other fabulous settings, my clearest memory is of a game we played untiringly. It came down to a thinly disguised worry - or joyful anticipation - about choosing a partner in marriage, or being chosen...or not being chosen. None of us had failed to notice, though we did not speak of it, that there was often a woman friend around at the Graces' hospitality, elegant and helpful and not quite equal. An old maid. We had better find somebody. We had better be found. We did not fantasize the appearance of our swains so much as what they would do, which would, in turn, define how our life would go.

Martha Allen's place was also on Long Island. Her handsome father, Fred Allen, had a legendary college athletic record in rowing - or maybe in all sports. I believe he was a banker, but it didn't show; I idolized him. Fred Allen was married to an engagingly natural socialite from St. Louis - almost a contradiction in terms to snobbish New York society - but she would not have cared. She had three brothers, all tall, loquacious, fun-making. The immoderate marble halls of the house were wholly mollified by a picture of Mrs. Allen by John Singer Sargent and a stream of young men who came to court the Allen's three fair daughters or talk to Fred Allen. At mealtime, there was never a servant in sight; everyone seemed to help without being burdened. The Catlin brothers would rise and make long toasts while the food got cold, telling stories more earthy than customary, and so eliciting warm laughter.

Martha came and went without supervision; we tagged along. She had a Sealyham aptly called Fatty, which expressed Martha's disdain of formalities. At any moment she could go off "to find Fatty." It was on the Allens' trees, so close to New York City, that I learned to swing birches, a rough and scratchy ride that made me feel in-the-know when we studied Robert Frost's poems at college. *One can do worse than be a swinger of birches.* Everyone loved to tease Martha for her elusive style; she was a will-o'-the-wisp. It was exhilarating to be Martha's friend, but it is always hard to keep up with a will-o'-the-wisp! I did not try, I

13

could not try to imitate Martha; I tried to stay centered in my own identity, but from her I learned a permissible independence that I used later in political situations when it seemed both wise and just to disregard conformity - but with gaiety, rather than anger.

Neither of our best friends was at all interested in student government, and neither played games like basketball or field hockey - that is, team games - which I loved. Betty thought them boyish, and Martha was too much an individualist. Neither considered formal education after Chapin's twelfth year. Both had coming-out parties. Both married extremely handsome men - two brothers - whom they did not meet at coming-out parties. Betty died early, although life expectancy is surely tuned to history and geography. I was far away in California - more than geography - so very far from the lovely times we four childhood friends had shared. It was hard for me to comprehend that money could not save her life.

Martha's husband is an artist. I seem to remember that Mrs. Allen did not think this a promising profession - in spite of the Sargent hanging on the wall. To Martha, this was not a matter of concern, not for one moment. Decades later, her husband is still painting and teaches art at a boys' prep school - which must be a lovely place for Martha to be whoever she now wants to be. Their son is a photographer and an artist. Like his father, he works in oil and watercolor; they present their work together in notable art galleries. A neighbor in New Hampshire writes, "They are all talented, beautiful and gracious - a fairybook family." Dear Martha, always...still! I have dwelled on *Low Country*, a volume of photographs by Tom Blagden, Jr. - "celebrating the essence of wilderness embodied in the rivers, forests, swamps, marshes and barrier islands of South Carolina." He sees so much more than I saw, but I am grateful to see now through the eyes of this son of an old friend.

Every few years in the 1920s and 1930s, my parents took staterooms on an ocean liner bound for Calais or Cherbourg or Bremerhaven. Sometimes we went along; Lawrance stayed home and was worried about. We played shuffleboard, figured miles out of laps around the deck, were spoiled with morning cups of bouillon, admired the sailors' bell-bottom trousers and longed for younger playmates than those who reclined in steamer chairs with blankets. We stared shyly at the passengers in steerage going west, imagining them the newest immigrants with high hopes, and those going east, perhaps suffering disillusionment or maybe sorrow to be leaving a loved one behind in the New World. First Class life aboard these wave-borne hotels - The Normandy, The Bremen, The Queen Mary - was not like the sea journeys of our ancestors, but the vastness and power of the ocean revealed itself during six days without sight of stick or stone or leaf. We felt a genuine excitement to see land when it appeared above the cliffs of Dover, Cherbourg, Bremerhaven. When winter palled on Manhattan Island, the streets strewn with salt and banked with dirty snow that did not melt, my parents joined a lavish club in Boca Raton on the Atlantic coast of Florida. It was a place of Moorish splendor, a romantic stage unsurpassed, flawed only by being beyond reach of any young man who might be inclined to go traveling with his mom and dad. I took one lesson from the famous golfer, Tommy Armour, fell in love and drove the ball so soaringly that I thought I had found my way out. By the second lesson I had lost the virtuosity of my natural swing and had to continue my search for a way of life I could believe in, without the help of any defining talent.

1931 was a very hard year for my mother. I learned what "hard" looks like; my life had been, and continues to be, so devoid of tragedy that I must strive to truly experience the world. Her father and her brother died in close succession. My father, Judge, went down to Street & Smith Publishing Company (my mother's family's business) to help steady the boat, especially for all who had worked long hours out of long years in the old red brick building. Judge was not a publisher at all, but he had a way of recognizing good people who would keep the presses rolling until the crisis could be resolved. However, other Smiths arrived at breakneck speed and not driving very carefully. Genetically speaking, the dynamo was the father-in-law of an adopted Smith son; the deleterious behavior had an outsider feeling.) My father withdrew, his efforts not appreciated, his motives misconstrued. Shortly after, he suffered a heart attack. My mother could not bear to attribute his illness to a thankless experience with her side of the family. It seems her father, whom she idolized, had not managed well. There were hints of a dummy company in Canada.

This sounded erotic to me, but "everybody was doing it." Such a question would not have been discussed in front of the children. I have nothing to tell. She took great care of Judge, and care for heart attacks was not like it is today. He was prescribed a regimen of absolute immobility to allow the lesser blood vessels to grow and pinch-hit for the damaged artery. He was not allowed to lift a hand from the covers, not even to hold a cigarette! The consequences of this prescription nearly killed him, but he escaped at last.

My parents then bought a house on Sanibel Island in the Gulf of Mexico. Here was a little village of fishermen and a few wealthy northern originals who disliked Miami. My mother took her art materials to the public school - one school including white and black children; her growing appreciation of all children could find expression here through many little portraits given away to pleased parents. My father spent a lot of time on a fishing boat, at ease in the company of skippers - hired - drifting on the sea, hoping for a run of tuna - not passionately.

I visited my parents on Sanibel Island. There was a white beach where the waves were so gentle they did not break the shells. The house had a blue-tiled roof, terrazzo floors and bougainvillea vines with orange and magenta leaves. Judge and Dorothy loved their house so much, they gave it a name, *Techado Azul*, and these were the first Spanish words I ever learned, although I had grown up in New York City with its huge Hispanic population; at Chapin we studied Latin and French. Assessing such incredible provincialism with an overglaze of class allows me to know the existence of walls between people. I did not stay long on Sanibel Island. It seemed to undermine my fervor. I would not look for people there; this paradise belonged to my parents. I would not pursue my Holy Grail at their gate. I wonder about this now. Did I believe that injustice was so pervasive - and never to be squared off - that each human being *must* address it as his or her own lot, in the blank page of personal opportunity within her or his own play?

When I was not militantly engaged in defining my own truths, however, I felt very comfortable with my mother, very close. She was frail with a brittle-bone disease since her childhood, probably attributable to a surely very expensive infant-feeding fad provided by her mother who suffered from hypochondria. As children, we were frequently warned, "Don't bump into your mother!" and this worked so well that it lingered on as, "Don't worry your mother!" which is more political. Dorothy Smith Holmes was indomitable, in a helpless sort of way. She expected herself to give orders. She rang for things. She wanted me to do this when I visited her, and I refused, it now seems gracelessly. After all, bad manners at home is not a useful way of changing the pitiless social structure of current society. I loved talking with my mother...about myself. (She was not at liberty to talk about herself; she was married.)

As a child, when I was sick, I wanted only her to do for me and raged against my father's decree that a "trained nurse" be hired to relieve her. Many times I have thought of her since, a parent without the back-up of antibiotics, which came upon the market just in time to lower my own children's scary fevers. Such life-sustaining drugs are still not available to most mothers of the world. Of course, one must not approach child health by the drug road. Assuring pure drinking water, universally, is probably a better way to start saving children...and providing enough food. Hunger is unconscionable. I have read that half of the seventy thousand child deaths occurring each day in the world are preventable. In Bangladesh alone, each year, hundreds of thousands of children die of diseases for which inexpensive vaccines and preventative intervention exist. The next best way would be to abjure war. Now in the '90s I support a woman's right to choose - not only her right to an abortion but her right to protect the child she bears and to be supported in her choices by readily available - ever improved - contraception. I relate to women leading antiwar demonstrations.

My mother was my witness; I tested my groping in the mirror of her mothering pride; sometimes a mother's biased reflection is downright annoying, but sometimes it is of inestimable solace. I did not want to be like her. She was not a useful role model for someone like me who had a journey to make. I did not want to ring for things!

Timothy asked the other day, "Where did your money come from? Where did it go?" The questions were appropriate. As the eldest child, it was her job to keep the family chronicles. I

17

thought I had answered those questions many times over. Maybe she did not know because I did not want to tell, but I do now. My mother's mother came East from Pittsburgh to marry George Campbell Smith, second-generation scion of the Street & Smith Publishing Company, which produced pulp magazines. In his book, *The Fiction Factory*, aptly named, Quentin Reynolds tells the story of these two young men, Street and Smith, who, "reaching out to newly immigrant readers with simple stories of romance and sports and adventure and mystery - *Love Story, Western Story, Detective Story, Nick Carter* and many others...knew what the masses wanted to read. They wanted to read of girls pursued (but never quite caught) by villains, of poor boys who managed to overcome all obstacles to achieve success...and stories in the virtue-must-triumph school that held out hope to the overworked, underpaid shop-girls that Prince Charming would come along." I thank Quentin Reynolds for his book and for publishing the following poem, My Ambition, by my great, great, uncle, Francis Shubael Smith, writing in the 1880s. (Reynolds reports that one of Francis's eleven brothers and sisters was called Freelove, and she traveled with her husband to California in a covered wagon!) Indeed, his "muse may be rude" - not so rude as more ingenuous than contemporary muses. I am glad this song is in my heritage.

> If I can any pleasure give
>   To those who daily labor
> If I can send one ray of joy
>   To any lowly neighbor
> 'Tis all the recompense I ask -
>   I labor for no other -
> In any man, however poor,
>   I recognize a brother.
> If I can cheer an aching heart
>   However poor and lonely
> Though rude my muse and plain my verse
>   My mission still is holy.
> And I care nothing for the sneer
>   Of pompous schools and classes
> So that I reach the heart and win
>   The plaudits of the masses.

I acknowledge other word-mixers in our family tree. Somewhere among my books a slender volume has lingered, *Fugitive Poems Make A Happy Landing* by Cora Gould Smith. I remember a wizened little old lady - probably of the age I now am - who lived in the Plaza Hotel on the south end of Central Park where sleepy old horses in straw hats dozed, waiting to give nostalgic couples a ride through Central Park in hansom cabs. Cora Smith Gould had one son whom she idolized. I remember that love and the Plaza Hotel...and smile.

I take down her book to find a few lines to honor her. She apparently had some personal connection with Oglethorpe University because she speaks of representative items entombed in a crypt beneath the administration building, not to be opened until A.D. 8113. "In the year of our Lord 1942, six thousand years is quite a long distance to reflect on." Cora Smith Gould could not have imagined the scope of humanity's genius in devising means of self-destruction! Can we even reach 2,000! In her acknowledgements, the poet thanks "the many editors who paved the way for whatever success I may have attained on the lyric trail." From her book, I will quote two stanzas from *Sunshine and Shadow* about early widowhood.

> Mother sits on a grassy knoll.
> So pitiful in black.
> Vain longings crying in her soul,
> "Dear heart, come back, come back!"
> Partly, the darlings sense her grief
> Shyly they meet her eyes.
> Bravely she smiles to their relief,
> Though lifeless, father lies.

In the succeeding generation, Street & Smith was a financial success, but my mother was determined to be an upwardly mobile reader; she did not read the pulps and did not display their much-discussed covers on her coffee table in the living room. She read classical and current novels like Henry Adams' *Mont Saint Michel et Chartres*. Slender volumes of poetry rested on her bedside shelf - Edna St. Vincent Millay, Eleanor Wylie, John Masefield. She did not learn the names of writers, including Theodore Dreiser, who were being paid - underpaid, but paid - for written words downtown at Street & Smith.

When I was a student at Bennington College in Vermont, I came down to Street & Smith in New York City to interview Daisy Bacon, editor of the enormously popular *Love Story*. Daisy Bacon apologized to no one for the caliber of her writers - especially not to a literature major who attended a private, experimental college on money produced in large part by her editorial acumen. She advised me that I dare not assume it was easy to write for *Love Story*. I was impressed by Daisy Bacon. She respected her readers. She was not exploiting them; she was one with them. I did not submit a story. Ceremonially, in my seventy-sixth year, I will try to write one.

In the same period of my life, I studied in the library of my mother's brother, George C. Smith, Jr. Although he had an executive desk at Street & Smith, he spent most of his time as a serious collector of rare books and first editions including works by Mark Twain and William Blake. He could afford to be. George had designed and set into a wall of his library a little scene showing Samuel Clemens piloting a riverboat. I also remember a reproduction of the Blake drawing, "I Want..." that was featured. Choosing this drawing did not express George's desire for more worldly goods; he had access to everything. George suffered the same bone infirmity as my mother; he walked with a slight limp that, deceptively, made him look a little pompous. As children, George and Dorothy had been artists together, doing meticulous copies of any pictures that came their way. To this companionship I attribute my mother's gift for "getting a likeness" in her portraits, to the delight of parents and the envy of perhaps more creative painters. Uncle George wore beautiful clothes. He owned a yacht to cruise on Long Island Sound and to dock on Manhattan's East River. For this pastime he wore white flannels, a nautical blue jacket, and a captain's hat. I was invited to sea on his boat, but I never found my way beneath his family smile. Speaking of family, a bachelor, he liked to say "great nuts from little acorns grow." His was a lonely eccentricity. My father seemed suspicious of every woman who went out with him. Why? I wonder if he thought George was gay and in his logic assumed these glamorous women sought George only for his money. I don't know. I liked George; maybe his friends liked him, too.

My mother's much younger sister shared George's humor. Anne was temporarily married to Jerry Wendon, allegedly a British cavalry officer, when they visited us at the Adirondack camp. Jerry was very daring; presumably he had done better with horses than with motorboats because he toppled over into the water and his legs were cut by the propeller of the motorboat he was about to ride. He was rushed by launch to the doctors, and returned with great bandages and noble sayings in his British accent. Assuring us it was not our fault, he allowed Aunt Anne to wait on him for the entire visit. Anne married four times, but her central passion was her interest in Mary, Queen of Scots.

I wrote Anne when I was deep into my roots phase. She told me about her travails in arranging a modus vivendi for her fourth husband, stricken with a debilitating illness. Anne was faithful and true, but she kept her account light. "Gypsy Rose Lee's father patted me on the seat as I went by his wheelchair. One of the old gals cried shame! but I'm afraid I turned round and gave him a grin. He didn't have much fun in that dreary place."

After this story, Anne made short shrift of my question. "Family history is all right if you don't search it out to find a title, like poor Aunt Cora did. She found one, all right. Sir Ralph Sadler. When I went to England one summer, she asked me to try to find a 'life' of Sir Ralph. I found one, and reading it felt a quite unholy delight in the fact that he married his laundress. I gave Aunt Cora the book. She thanked me and that was that. We never spoke of it again. Aunt Cora had an oil painting of Sir Ralph with a falcon on his wrist. The portrait had once been full length but she cut it off at the knees because he was bow-legged. When I saw it, it was in an oval frame. Her son remarked that if you go back far enough, you can find anything you want. I don't doubt it." Still, it was Anne who gave me pictures of my ancestor, Caroline von Westphalen, who fell in love with Christian Schmertz, a commoner and felt obliged to emigrate to America...*ausgevanderr nach Amerika im 1833.*

My mother's ancestors, Christian Schmertz and Carolyn von Westphalen. Carolyn was forced to leave European society because she fell in love with a "commoner." They moved to America.

Artemas Lawrance Holmes and his wife, Mary Bloomer Holmes.
My father's ancestors were in the ministry.

My father's parents - Artemas Henry Holmes and Lillian Stokes Holmes (self portrait).

My mother's parents, Annie Kemmerer Schmertz and George Campbell Smith, of Street and Smith Publishing.

My mother, Dorothy Smith Holmes, saw great change in her lifetime.

My father, Artemas "Judge" Holmes, playing tennis on the Riviera.

CHAPTER THREE

Judge and Dot

My paternal grandmother had a more substantive "disability." With faithful regularity, the twins were taken to see their Grandmother Holmes. I remember the twisted, paralyzed and delicate hands with which she managed to paint a ravishing self-portrait in a flowered taffeta dress. So fine was the work that it was suggested the picture had been done by her loyal care-giver - but would not this have been equally amazing? In my recollection, Lillian Holmes bends attentively toward us, offering a cookie and inviting us to talk with her parrot. Preceding her in death, her husband, Artemas Holmes, had been a New York lawyer who bought and lived in one of the Villard houses, now a historical landmark east of St. Patrick's Cathedral.

My father's given name was also Artemas, and we learned to spell it "right." He had been nicknamed "Judge" as a child because his face did not seem to smile, but he was good-natured and popular with all sorts of people who used his moniker at first meeting, thinking he was a judge. To us it seemed as if he was on first-name terms with the whole world. In his youth he was a minor tennis champion, winning at singles and mixed-doubles in southern France. He had shelves of cups and trophies, which my mother polished frequently until at last a product came along that could keep them tarnish-free and glowing as only silver gleams. Judge played the many courts of Europe. He was once the Riviera lawn tennis doubles champion. He was a handsome bachelor in great demand socially - a "tennis bum," as he put it. There is a story that when some players were stumbling over protocol in the presence of Swedish royalty, Judge said, "The King and I will take on you two," and settled the problem. His behavior was untrammeled by pretense. He insisted on playing to win, but he was never out of control, never angry at his partner's gaffes or his own, always courteous, always drily amusing. His tennis game was cerebral, compensating for a rather stiff musculature in an athlete. It drove my brother crazy years later, plunging from side to side, to the net and back in pursuit of Judge's ball.

At his death, my mother received a flood of sorrowing mail. *Of all my friends, no one could be more irreplaceable...fine, gentle and of such rectitude...quaint, amusing, affectionate friend.*

Paradoxically, in the realm of ideas, my father was not an intellectual and did not enjoy discussions with me; he could not play the game with words. Unlike many of his friends, he did not become vitriolic about President Roosevelt, but no more than they did he notice that the WPA and other government programs were saving the golden goose. However, my father made no snide remarks about the hapless victims of economic dislocation "leaning on their shovels" - shovels that surely did not fit their hands. Today, in 1992, when I stand in a long line to mail a package from Ukiah, I am entertained by a fine mural on the post office wall, done by an artist of the WPA, leaning on his shovel.

Judge liked to boast about reading his "one-book-of-the-year." My mother loved him more than books, more than her considerable artistic talent, more than her children. She had promised that she would always have child care in place so that she could go out with him. When I observe the fraught young parents today, I think Judge had a clue for a strong marriage: child care in place. If the economy requires that both parents work, funds for quality child care must be provided, at least as much as supports our soldiers. Soldiers are our children once removed! Conservative politicians who proclaim family should remember this in their budgets!

My father's philosophy about my decision to attend the fledgling Bennington College, in which my mother's friends, Mrs. Franklin and Mrs. Webb, were importantly involved and for which he would pay handsomely, times two for twins, was, "All right, but don't take anything seriously." At the time I did not appreciate this Polonius's advice, and today I still don't...but maybe I will tomorrow. In retrospect, I imagine he feared we would catch disqualifiers, and he would be unable to marry us off.

Sunday morning throughout the winter my father would head for The Racquet Club for some squash - a game played by bouncing a little ball off the walls, no woman's eye would ever see, since no woman was admitted to this male enclave. Occasionally he would play a rubber of bridge with Eli Culbertson, whose name was synonymous with a recently formalized system for communicating with a partner about the bidding...in lieu of eyebrow signals or a swift kick under the table. My father's Sabbath occupations left my mother free to take us to church. First we attended St. James Episcopal Church, a block to the south of our home. I enjoyed the pageantry as priests in gorgeous vestments moved the golden cross down the aisle followed by choirboys with angels' voices, tenors, baritones, basses - the whole tonal spectrum of male sound approaching where I stood in the pew, passing, disappearing into the sanctuary.

A few years later, my mother shifted her support to the Madison Avenue Presbyterian Church, a few blocks north. It was here that a young Scottish preacher interpreted the New Testament in a way that profoundly affected my life. Dr. George Buttrick, at the pulpit of a parish that cut across the socio-economic spheres expressed in the layout of New York City, preached to the rich, making manifest the message of Jesus, lest anyone dare to misunderstand just because the hymn tunes were familiar and the stained-glass windows filtered the harsh light. During the week he ministered to the poor through visitation and through the many organizations initiated by his wife and parishioners. It confounds me that it never occurred to me to join one of these. Living three stories up above the earth, I identified with no neighborhood - but I did hear. A few years ago, I sat in a church in El Salvador listening to just such a preacher. My glance fell on the earnest faces of the young people. "Be ye sheep of the Lord, but be ye also shepherd. Care about the world!" This "liberation theology" was a dangerous message in El Salvador, and would have been dangerous on Madison Avenue in New York City during the Depression of the '30s, if it had been listened to as literal rather than poetic truth.

In 1991 in Taos, New Mexico, where I had traveled to a few concerts performed by my second daughter, Holly, the better to hear her with, I entered a lovely adobe church. The sacrament of

Holy Communion was in progress, and I was moved to share in the ritual of little chunks of white bread and tiny goblets of grape juice. *Do this in remembrance of me.* The historical reality became achingly clear: Revolutionary friends have supper together. Don't forget! In the impending dismay, the ghastly punishment, don't forget what we talked about. As the congregation filed out, the minister sought me - a new face. During the brief minute of our conversation, we came upon the name of George Buttrick, "one of the finest preachers of the Protestant church." So, he has not been forgotten! I believe he entered his Gethsemene when he prayed for the Japanese during the dark days of World War II. He lost his pulpit while he was engaged in his calling, Christianity!

By then I was in California, living in a beachside room, with the sand at my door and the blue Pacific in my window - Rosie the Riveter or, more accurately, Ellie the Electrician. It had not yet been decided who would win the war. It was after Pearl Harbor, of which President Roosevelt had said, "This day will live in infamy!" But how about Executive Order 9066?

I do not recall feelings of hostility toward Japanese Americans. Russell, my husband to be, had pointed out the deserted farms on the La Brea flats; their erstwhile owners had treated him graciously when he came as a novice insurance salesman to collect their payments. Did I ask where they had gone? It is not as if I were uneducated; I had just come from Philadelphia, where I had known loyal German Americans who fell under random suspicion because of Hitler. Why did I not recognize that President Roosevelt's Executive Order 9066 was issued in appalling disregard of the United States Constitution! Oh, sure I pulled down my shades and taped the edges lest telltale light escape across the Pacific Ocean. But why did I not speak out against the incarceration of Japanese Americans? I read the particulars in an American Civil Liberties publication (Jan-Feb 1992) Bitter Memories, 50th Anniversary of the Internment Order.

> Within a matter of weeks, 110,000 Japanese Americans were forcibly evacuated from their West Coast homes and sent to remote internment centers...one of the most desolate was Tule Lake, a bleak and barren volcanic plateau just south of the

Oregon border. 18,000 Japanese Americans were interned there in rows of tar-paper shacks...the conditions were harsh, this lead to strikes, violence and martial law. (When an ACLU director went to investigate and publicize the conditions, he was ordered off the premises, and the non-welcome reinforced by the putting of two sacks of salt in his gas tank, causing a stop-and-go trip the 400 miles back to San Francisco.

I know that there were many-years-belated apologies and some compensation. One cannot truly reverse what happened, but one can be altered in remembering this racist act perpetrated by our nation even as we were sending our youth abroad to fight fascism. Each one of us, as onions, must peel away layers of racism!

Recently I watched the film *Come See Paradise* with Tamlyn Tomita and Dennis Quaid. In this, the Japanese American citizens were housed at a race track, in barns, from which the horses were being hastily removed. Behavior in an "emergency" turns up the baleful corners of the human soul, rationalizing (as Bob Dylan sings) that we have God on our side.

It was Dorothy Holmes who took Ruth and me to church, but also to the little art galleries along Madison Avenue where we learned to recognize form expressed through subject matter, and to enjoy both in a canvas on the wall. She took us to concerts for the best of reasons: she loved to go herself. Saturday mornings, we attended the celebrated Children's Concerts at Carnegie Hall, led by Ernest Schelling. We became aware of Toscanini in the world, marveled at the virtuosity of a twelve-year-old Yehudi Menuhin, adored Paul Robeson. With my mother, we felt the magical promise in the slowly rising curtain, the rigid asbestos curtain first that, whatever environmental damage it may have been doing, was there to control fire and introduce the silken curtain with its drapery-folds lifted at last revealing life on the stage of which we would momentarily become a part. Katherine Cornell in *Alien Corn*, Clare Luce and Fred Astaire in *Gay Divorcee*, Lillian Hellman's *Children's Hour*, the black musical, *Green Pastures*, Burgess Meredith in *Winterset*. *Tobacco Road, Otello, La*

29

Boheme, Aida, The Mikado, The Marriage of Figaro, the whole *Wagner Ring* - these are a few that cross my mind with chronological disregard. For our twins' tenth birthday party, my mother took our whole class to Barnum & Bailey's Circus, but it was in the Broadway theaters that my mother could participate in life beyond the precinct of her adored husband's tennis and bridge games. I am ever grateful. This was my mother's contribution - not entirely unknowing - to the development of a radical mind. For me, a fund of experience was laid by, shaped by the most vibrant of art forms. I grew up thinking that the theater bill was more newsworthy than the headline litany of murders and elections. If preachers and painters and playwrights wanted to speak, we were there with my mother to listen.

My mother with her children, Lawrance, Ruth and Prudence Anne.

Kate Mannix, of County Clare, with us at St. Jean de Luz.

The twins, Ruth Hilda and Prudence Anne.

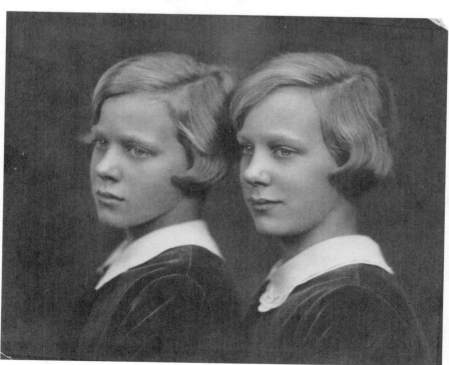

Kate and the twins - Lawrance and his nanny, Bea.

ELLIS ISLAND
1892–1992
TM © 1987 SL/EIF, INC.

The Statue of Liberty-Ellis Island Foundation, Inc.

proudly presents this

Official Certificate of Registration

in

THE AMERICAN IMMIGRANT WALL OF HONOR

to officially certify that

KATE MANNIX

who came to America from

COUNTY CLARE

is among those courageous men and women who came to this country in search of personal
freedom, economic opportunity and a future of hope for their families.

Lee A. Iacocca
The Statue of Liberty-Ellis Island
Foundation, Inc.

LIBERTY
1886·1986

My brother, Lawrance, was a novelist.

My namesake, Anne Smith Wendon, an ambulance driver in World War I.

It's one of us!

CHAPTER FOUR

Kate

However, in earlier childhood I was closer to another, and I learned that these two women had the probability of hurting each other, given their incompatible bailiwicks, living in the same household, bonded by love for the children and separated by *class*.

My Earth Mother was Kate Mannix. She was our Irish nurse. Kate was one of the daring or desperate young women who left their homes in Ireland and, with their courage in their pockets, and perhaps little else, walked up the gangplank of a ship out of Liverpool bound for New York Harbor. Now, with adventurous children of my own, now that I am so much older than she was when she took care of us, I think of Kate. I look back at her, where once I looked up into her red-cheeked face and laughing eyes. I hear her voice, her endearing brogue. Did she leave her cottage in the spring with the *"wild Irish rose a-bloomin'"* that she loved to sing about? Did her new shoes scuff along a dusty road or her skirts billow in *"a jaunting cart"*? Was it as hard for her as it was for Danny Boy who *"heard the pipes a-callin"*? Did her father tell her that it would *"not be her beauty alone"* that would make people love her, but *"the truth in her eyes ever shinin"*? Did a homesick boy in New York City offer, *"I'll take you home again, Kathleen, across the ocean wild and wide"*? Did a boy from home plead, *"Come back to Erin, Mavourneen, Mavourneen!"*? Having heard so much about Kate, our children presented us in our seventieth year with a trip to Ireland, County Clare. I still love the old Irish songs, but I am more likely to play a cassette of the music of Siamsa, the National Folk Theatre of Ireland.

A snapshot taped to my wall, as if for just a day, shows Kate, tall in long, white skirts and a broad-brimmed, navy straw hat; proudly she holds her twins by the hand. How she told us

34

stories! Ruth remembers one about "the little people" - she did not call them leprechauns - who would push a man off the bridge on his way home, not explicitly from the pub, but on a moonless night. We treasure a letter Kate sent to Ruth to comfort her when her baby was "overdue." Only a small part of it reads, "You shall probably find the little one swimming in glorious happiness in a pond watered by soft April showers - and reflected in these waters beautiful and varied crocuses growing gaily on its banks. What an enchanting time for your baby to appear in the midst of such tokens of love and power and glory of the magnificent Creator." We learned to talk at Kate's knee!

I can see her standing at the ironing board, tears streaming down her cheeks because her twins would sometime soon be removed from her care. How would I feel if it were decreed that my bairns would be graduated from my motherhood! Of course, at some point they have been, but in a mysterious facet of nature's way, a minute before the moment, one is ready to hear it, ready oneself for a new life unencumbered by apron strings.

Kate allowed us to feel that we were her whole life, but I wonder now. Did she have a mother in "the auld country" who walked a piece of the way with her and then turned back to the cottage weeping, but knowing there was one less mouth to feed? Did Kate arrive at Ellis Island all alone, or was the substantial and well-organized Irish community ready to receive her? I know she was friends with a member of "New York's finest" who directed traffic at the intersection of Park and Seventy-second, below our window. I believe she had uncles "on the force." Did Tammany Hall monitor her vote? With us, Kate had one day off a week and one evening, "when possible." I never wondered, did Kate make love? Was there some rule that this could not happen on our premises or on "our time"? I am under the impression that she was well paid. My parents would have thought so; they did not cut this sort of corner, but the prevailing opinion of what "green labor" was worth was undoubtedly not "union." Domestic workers have always had a hard time organizing because they "live in," and thus seem to be part of others' families. Kate appeared to buy into this idea and I did, too. I was totally surprised when Kate became the nurse of another child, the little boy who grew up to be Congressman Hamilton Fish.

Kate exchanged letters with me and Ruth for many years. Her handwriting was gracefully florid and, as years went by, looped up inextricably into the words on the line above. While she was with us and forever after, she scanned the society pages and compared notes with other nurses as they sat on Central Park benches, rocking perambulators or keeping an eye on little children at play. Why not? She knew more about life on and off those pages than I...and cared more. I did not want to grow to be a "child-care worker" but I envied her earthy, lyrical "Irishness"...it seemed to me, she and hers had more fun than "my people."

And then the dreaded day arrived when Kate was fired. I can see the richly appointed room in a hotel off the Champs Elysees near the Arc de Triomphe. I can feel the blue velvet on an armchair. It was raining in Paris, a summer rain. We were told that Kate would be leaving us here; kindly, we had brought her this far on her way to "her home" in Erin; she would be rejoining "her people" across the English Channel; an English governess would take her place, a lady more able to show us ways we would now need to know. Kate was for childhood, Miss Potter was for ladyhood! I knew Kate was sad to be going. I knew this was not her choice. "Her people" were us - in New York! I could have fought for her, no matter if to no avail, but I already had some inkling of where my life was slated to go. I was not prepared to challenge that or plead to live forever in the nursery. I don't remember any farewell embrace, any last touch. I cried into the blue velvet cushions. That was sixty years ago.

In 1989, Ruth and I participated in registering the name of KATE MANNIX FROM COUNTY CLARE on the American Immigrant Wall of Honor. It was part of the Statue of Liberty-Ellis Island Restoration Project, chaired by Lee Iacocca. His letter reads in part, "All names registered will appear on public display at Ellis Island as a testament to the heroism and triumphs your family experienced in coming to America for the first time. The many thousands of visitors will recognize and respect your family's role in fulfilling the American dream of hope, freedom and opportunity for all." We sent a copy to the Mannix family in Ireland, but I do not know if anyone was there to receive it.

At seventy-five, autobiography is not a linear vision; the line would be too long; it would get tangled as when a fisherman casts too boldly across a rough stream. Fisher_person_! At seventy-five, biography is magically entertained, concentric for the most part, a multidimensional blend of landscape, portraiture, film clip, a drift of popular tunes with time-cued lines - "Brother, can you spare a dime?" - "I left my heart at the stage door canteen" - stage dialogue, a moving figure, familiar but not exactly as one sees oneself reflected in a store window, a bunch of dates scrawled illegibly on a United Nations Children's Calendar or simply recalled with a special person who, for me, would be my twin.

A penny-postcard arrived..."Health news - I don't know why I have always shared with you hard news, but I always have and thank you, my dear, as my little grandson would say. My cat-scan says I do have cancer...what can I say except I intend to continue living good - do all my same things." Ruth's writing was a code conveying her rapture in her busy life, including the defiant misuse of the adverb. She wrote, "I still don't know if I have a future but I've decided for all our sakes one doesn't ask. I'm trying to enjoy each moment."

Somewhere I read that if we live long enough, we'll all get cancer. Is this normal, then, for beings on this earth, a natural imperfection - even among the lilies of the field - that is ultimately lethal? Or have we relatively recent human beings polluted a prior perfection? I ask my Native American friends, if the design was perfect, why were we allowed to spoil it all - the only creature dangerous to creation and itself? They do not respond to this question. They know they did not spoil it all.

Ruth gave her answers to questions about life through what she did. She was a faithful wife. She raised six children. She would have believed each person's story a valid and a valuable one. For herself, she needed to take part in a construct beyond motherhood. Essentially an artist, she chose a site of profound symbolism: prison. She and a friend, Marni Henretig, an advocate with the Pennsylvania Prison Society, developed a toy room - more like a closet - where incarcerated fathers could bring their visiting children, choose a toy and play. It was much better than having the kids run wild, while parents, knee to knee, held hands miserably in a crowded room. The scene made no individual judgments, but seemed to question the concept of incarceration.

Ruth said, "In our home we do not punish. Surely, I picked up a young child and carried him/her to his/her room, believing that, whatever behavior was going on was saying, 'This child needs to be alone.' We did not remove privileges - maybe used the more powerful voice - did not demean. Children felt the pressure of high assumed expectations. I cannot believe that placing men in long-term custody in an impossible environment is going to prepare them for life outside."

A prisoner joked, "With Ruth Bacon, there is no unemployment!" Another said, "She treated all the men as friends."

Ruth said, "The Parent Child Resource Center at Graterford Prison functions as a gift from the leadership group of men to their fellow inmates, who in turn can provide this pleasure to their families, and above all to the children. As leaders, the men model respect, intelligence, expertise, and craftsmanship by relating directly to the children through supporting the father role by giving out supplies, games, and age-appropriate toys, and through modeling the validity of men interacting with children. Teaching at its best is giving to each child what that child needs to grow, be it information or a listening presence." Ruth did this.

Where was I? From whence did I first engender ideas for improving my economic status, my class, downward? Inclining to the modern theory that everything defining happens in the early years before one is in any position to do anything about it, I have courted my childhood memories for whatever stories might show up to explain me. Now I will pretend to marshal a few facts. I attended a private school that eventually located its buildings not among its likely applicants, but on cheaper land near the East River. The drive across town provided a daily lesson for children riding in the family limousine, with a lap-robe, kicked off their knees, piloted past tenements by a uniformed chauffeur. In the ninth grade I wrote a composition about a hungry man watching the cooking of roasts through the street level window of a brasserie. "The lights blinked on and off like an eye red with weeping." I was awarded an "A" from the literature teacher, a grandly opulent woman with cigarette stains on her fingers, indecipherable layers of clothing, and an affirming style of appreciation that was well worth working for. I found ashes in the

38

pages of my homework - quite magical in that time before they might seem suicidal - and Mrs. Emerson's authentic writer's margin notes. It was Miss Stewart, who took us on bird walks - her province was all of nature, including live bodies, as well as dead ones which could be squeamishly dissected, especially frogs. It was clear Miss Stewart preferred them alive. I was later to learn in Stowell Round's book, *Men and Birds in South America*, that "bird watching" was a crucial navigational element for explorers before the discovery of the compass. Miss Meredith had all of history by heart, whereas I could retain none of it; it was not until I came across a socio-economic rather than military concept of history that I could remember that Alaric the Goth took Rome in 410, the Normans conquered England in 1066, 1616 Shakespeare slept, 1863 Lincoln freed the slaves. Was there any mention of the Bonus Marchers, Tent City, the Army of the Unemployed, or General MacArthur firing on veterans of World War I? Did we ever learn that the Civil War was an economic war and that black people carried out their own liberation? Did we begin to learn a new use of the alphabet, as in NRA, WPA, NLRB and CCC? Perhaps not but I am grateful to the school that harbored me for thirteen years.

To graduate from Miss Chapin's School for Girls, one had to memorize one hundred seemingly unrelated dates, some as mysterious as the Hegira, and add six columns of ten digits - aloud, standing before the Assembly. Two, seven, thirteen, twenty-one, thirty, thirty-seven, forty-two, forty-seven, forty-eight, fifty-seven...The performance was timed and surrounded with dread, but today I can survive without a pocket calculator. How was Miss Fairfax to imagine that the skill she demanded of us would soon be an anachronism? However, in retrospect, I realize that Miss Chapin and Miss Fairfax were women of inspired vision, as was Miss Ethel Stringfellow, a southern woman who they chose to take over the leadership of this New York City private school when they retired.

> "It will take many generations still to make the
> world an ideal place for our descendants to live in,
> but this one thing we must attempt."
> Maria Bowen Chapin

"Inheritor of a glorious past, each generation is a trustee for posterity. To preserve, protect and transmit this inheritance in its fullness is one of its highest duties."   Mary Cecelia Fairfax

"Undoubtedly the fostering of social interest and responsibility throughout their years has enabled our graduates to be leaders in so many worthwhile enterprises in the larger community."
                                        Ethel Grey Stringfellow

While I have discovered these statements of belief in an Alumnae Bulletin of 1991, there is no doubt that they resonated through the nascent consciousness of the little girls in the charge of these three extraordinarily committed women.

At Miss Chapin's, I had no clue that Lincoln declared himself more pro-union than abolitionist, that black people, at first, were not welcome to enlist in the army fighting for their liberation. Although I am still not one to extol military prowess, having read *The Negro's Civil War*, by James McPherson, I applaud the courage shown by determined black regiments. And, although it was going on, beyond my classroom, we never talked about an Aussie, Harry Bridges and his beloved rank-and-file, who were shutting down the port of San Francisco in order to win their own hiring hall; I would not have known why this even mattered!

CHAPTER FIVE

Bennington

It was at Bennington College that I met people who did not think the world revolved around New York City - and certainly not its private schools. This was liberating news. It took me awhile to comprehend the new pace; in French Literature, instead of being assigned 35 pages by Pierre Loti, we were advised to read all we could find of André Gide in the library, preferably in the original language, and be prepared to discuss. At Bennington I became fast friends with the daughters of a Jewish owner of a clothing factory, of a Philadelphia lawyer and of a founder of a progressive co-educational school where students and faculty had to grow their own food. Annie Meyers, Barbara Saul, Jean Hinton. With fond respect I speak their maiden names; our friendship has ebbed and flowed over the events of some fifty years, including their marriages and mine. Each had children - and I know their names. When I think of Annie, she is solicitously inquiring the thoughts of young children in a socio-psychiatric setting; a counselor to the future. Barbara, who has such a talent for helping people know each other and care, appears to me as the image of an ardent messenger around the United Nations building in New York City and no less among friends on Key West. Jean personifies the Putney School style - on the road to find four corners of the earth. I was moved to hear that recently, Jean, even sight-impaired and in her seventies, traveled alone all the way to Bolivia to support a friend in a political context. That is like her. However, I see her most clearly as we kayaked down the Connecticut River at dusk, apprehensively searching the banks for our appointed beach where we had left our car downstream, perilously close to a millrace. I see Jean as the guide of a skiing trip in Vermont, with accommodations in a generous farmer's barn; I avoided freezing by draping my shivering body around a patient cow's back. Jean taught me about adventure without money - unlike my parents' fabulous sorties. I chose such fine friends. Chicago, New York, Concord! These cities glow for me because my good friends live there.

At Bennington I met many people and attended to minds with brilliant memory for the written word. We were inspired by poets Genevieve Taggard, Leonie Adams, William Troy, Irving Fineman, Wallace Fowlie. We felt a personal pride as our professors held discourse with Clifton Fadiman and John Dewey. The little community of some three hundred women students, a few men expediently enrolled in the drama department, the faculty and staff of a new campus on a Vermont hillside, were challenged by Dr. Reinhold Niebuhr discussing "the resources and limitations of the democratic tradition of the present social crisis," and André Malraux speaking of the "thinking people and Spain." Ferdinand Bindel asked whether the "CIO served the American worker," Margaret Mead analyzed "temperament and culture in the South Seas," Grinnell Jones introduced the concept of "industrial chemistry as a creative science." Robert Frost stopped by to read at the Bennington Evening Meeting, as did Louise Bogan, Muriel Rukeyser, James Agee, and Archibald MacLeish. No wonder it was assumed that every single person would attend every event! The sounds of the harpsichord touched by Ralph Kilpatrick, the sounds of the four-stringed P'-Pa, its notation elucidated by Chinese artist Sophia Han, the unprecedented sounds of the Ether Wave, electrical music where Leon Theremin touched only the air, the sound of Leadbelly playing his poetry of the American Negro to an academic audience that included no black face - all opened the heart in a way that burst the wildest expectations. I have never felt so alive, so contemporary as I did during my four years at Bennington College. We were entranced to listen as our professors held discourse with visiting genius. I was educated; I was prepared to be whomever I might be...and to go on learning about the world till death do us part.

Taking turns freezing in the rumble seat of the little coupe our parents had given us, we took as many friends as possible and drove hours over treacherous snowy roads to Albany or New York City to hear Carl Jung, and then again to hear Thomas Mann read, and to hear Buckminster Fuller discuss the "economic responsibilities of invention." Sometimes we arrived too exhausted by weather to listen worthily. On the way to see Martha Graham dance in a garment such as had never been seen before, though now a well-known trademark, my car spun round on a patch of ice beneath the bulwarks of an underpass; no one smashed into us; we drove on. Today, I read Maggie Lewis in the Christian Science Monitor who quotes Martha Graham, "I did not dance the way that people danced. I had what I called a connection and release. I used the floor - I used the flexed foot. I showed effort. My foot was bare. I showed on stage what most people come to the theater to avoid." Dance was integral to Bennington, preparing me for my children - my youngest daughter, Laurel, and my daughter-in-law, Krissy Keefer, are both dancers, as are my little grandsons. But back then, at Bennington, I almost drowned in humility. I was repeatedly rescued by New England farmscapes, snowscapes, ski slopes and promises to a love, safely far away; my intended was a secretary to the United States ambassador in Japan. The thought of him kept me loyal to my books. When David returned - it was after my graduation - I was disappointed; he seemed to have no deep curiosity in the controversial aspects of America's Asian relationships, which would suddenly lead to the Japanese bombing of our fleet at Pearl Harbor. Of course, I did not imagine this at the time - and it is a matter of serious speculation today as to who did have reasons to anticipate this deadly outcome of "negotiations" still taking place in Washington up to December 7, 1941. But I expected David to have at least a passionate awareness of where he had been. I learned the expectation of "passionate awareness" at Bennington; it was a must. I was beginning to need a political viewpoint in order to relate to the world's conflagrations. They were not simply fires. Rain would not put them out.

I think it was here that David and I realized we would not spend history together, although we had spent so many adolescent/young adult years assuming that we would, looking only at each other. He made me feel that my questions were aggressive, an embarrassment to him in his position. He enrolled at Union Theological Seminary. Believing as I did then, and do today, that theology can either obscure or reveal the revolutionary

43

implications of Jesus' teachings, I did not assume our parting was derived from his study. But I did know; we both did. I phoned him when I came to New York City from the West Coast. He invited me to come to the service where he was preaching. He looked so fine in his surplice. I had seen his clerical collar years before, starched and buttoned backwards when he took off his coat to row on the Schuylkill River. I would dearly like to hear how life has gone on for the Reverend David McAlpine Pyle.

As time went on, my work at Bennington College was illuminated by studying with the well-loved professor of French literature, Wallace Fowlie. He was a young Bostonian in whom had emerged at the first hearing of the language, a devotion to everything French. He spoke as a native and wrote poetry in his adopted tongue, which must be the highest linguistic achievement. I could hear the depth of his entrancement as he read favorite texts to the dozen young women gathered around his table in the "red barn." His laughter forgave us for our limitations; his modesty included us.

In Wallace Fowlie's book, *Pantomime, A Journal of Rehearsals*, he wrote, "French was no longer a study for me, it was a mode of apprehension. French books were not like other books. They were gateways to a new universe of feeling and understanding. I discovered a vast and generous chance of beginning life all over again."

Wallace Fowlie was the first writer I had the privilege of knowing as friend. I spent a lot of time thinking about him - rather, in imaginary dialogue with him - as I walked along the country roads of Bennington, and felt happy.

In Paris, he stayed with Mme. Naomi Renan. The summer between my third and fourth year at Bennington, I went alone by ship to France and stayed in the student quartier of Mont St. Michel, and then moved to the home of Mme. Renan. I dined with her and her black-attired female companion, and tried my best to comprehend the contradictions of the extreme opposing forces that regularly passed through her home. She was the daughter of Ernst Renan, the renowned liberal philosopher, and mother of Charles Péguy, who extolled the right-wing phalanx of Catholicism, a soldier-poet consecrating the arts of war. I visited the galleries and discovered for myself the work of Georges Roualt in an out-of-the-way chapel outside Paris. I rented a car, *un vieux taco*, and went driving with Pierre Duvauchelles and his sister and Les Hussamedins, a Turkish brother and sister. I learned to laugh in French, and be companionable in French. "*Dites, elle désire une salle de bains! Pourquoi, mon vieux?*" How could I explain that I could not discover the word for "toilet"; it certainly was not a room to take a bath! They found me funny and surprising, and I had the car. They used colloquial speech, hard to find in my Petit Larousse; harder to understand than the lectures at the Sorbonne.

Finally, I joined Wallace Fowlie (who took the name Michel Wallace) for a literary pilgrimage to places celebrated by French authors. We spoke only French. He had written to me, "*Je cherche quelques coins tranquilles pour travailler, et je souhaite que nous puissions nous voir sous des cieux francaises. A bientot, Michel.*"

I loved Wallace Fowlie; he could not disappoint me, but my heart ached that our hands did never touch. To honor him best, I will quote his explication of the writer's fate.

> The will to write is a seizure and a frenzy. Everything else appears less imperative. But everything counts henceforth: every acquaintance, every gesture, every tree, every cup of coffee. It is impossible for a writer to waste time. The vaster his reservoir of memories and impressions, the more rigorously he will choose and synthesize. No mater how delirious and exalted is the experience he has directly, he will always think in terms of its ending and of its ultimate absorption into a work. The real delirium of any experience will be its transposition into art. No matter how involved he becomes with people, an artist never lives, he observes life. He is always suspended, and his personal suffering comes from the terrible truth that he is unable to participate in life without recording it, without stylizing it and adjusting it. To possess the temperament of an artist and to know deeply the dilemma of wanting to write about life without being able to know life directly...

In aged retrospect I recognize the prevalence of this dilemma throughout my life. My confusion in Normandy on a literary journey with Wallace Fowlie was simply that I was not yet a writer. My definition of a writer is shorter than his. A writer is someone who writes; but I will always cherish what seemed to me to be a grammatical smile: *Je souhaite que nous puissions nos voir.*

It was at Bennington College that Ruth and I parted in a significant way; I believe it was she who felt it was time. For two years we had shared a double room; it was Bennington's second and third year. I recall the determination of the fledgling institution that no rules be laid down until the need was manifest; one girl had a lamb down the hall whose little feet made such a clatter that a rule was made: no animals in the dorms.

Our twinship was still so natural that we could not comprehend why another girl would come over to our room to spend the valuable time-of-day or, as is said currently, to just hang out. We knew the pleasure of companionship, but not the need. At some point Ruth decided that if our parents were determined to give us a "coming-out party" at the River Club in New York City, she would accept the rare scenario in a genuinely appreciative way. She did not return to Bennington, lived at home, and participated in the whole social agenda. Incidentally, she attended classes at the Art Students' League.

Ruth was on a Quaker mission in Flint, Michigan, and taking a course at The Neue Bauhaus, when she met Ed Bacon. Then Ruth, the rebel, came home and delighted her father by agreeing to a large wedding in the garden of the Long Island home. Well! At least, one of us. Judge's generosity deserved more!

Ruth appears throughout my narrative, but not yet in her proudest role, that of mother. If she were looking over my shoulder, she would like me to type about her children. There is a Native American rumor that if you take a picture, you steal the soul. I hope the Bacons will not mind my briefest "snapshots", here. Karin designs festivals and rallies, giving much needed theatricality to the gatherings. Elinor has a real estate development company; recently she salvaged a tumbling down church and made it the centerpiece of an urban housing plan. Michael is a cellist and composes music enhancing the aesthetic of the silver screen. Hilda's training in physical therapy reaches way beyond her hospital clinic to serve the needs of the neighborhood. Kyra designs neighborhoods. Kevin is an actor, both "live" and on film.

These people grew up in downtown Philadelphia, a requirement of their father's job as City Planner. At the house on Locust Street was a large round dark-oak supper-table at which the Bacons could observe eachother at least once a day, as Ruth laid out the food she hastily assembled with cheerful spontaneity from the little mom-and-pop grocery stores on 21st Street; only rarely did she go inside a super-market. She was a creative short order cook.

There have been transcontinental exchanges between Ruth's children and mine...from Locust Street to the N3 Ranch. Ruth would love that her grand-daughter will apprentice at my daughter, Laurel's, theatre and dance school.

I accompany Marvin Breckinridge into the mountains, packing her photographic equipment. Today, she is still a supporter of the Frontier Nursing Service.

Ruth dancing with her daughter, Karin.

Biking in Austria in 1935.

CHAPTER SIX

Frontier Nursing Service

In the spaces between semesters at Bennington College, I volunteered at the Frontier Nursing Service in the Kentucky mountains. Here I met British nurse-midwives, working-class women who were part of a distinguished tradition - missionary or beloved colonialist - of health care pioneers who traveled forth to help people of other lands, especially within the British Empire and including North America. The daughter of a well-known Kentucky family, Mary Breckinridge, grieving in the tragic loss of her own two children, had chosen a ten-square-mile area of the Appalachians - so isolated that the people spoke with an Old English accent, their heritage. There she developed a midwifery-nursing model that could be adapted to similar conditions the world over. Her own model had been the work of Highlands and Islands Medical Nursing Service in Scotland, where she had studied while enrolled at the British Hospital For Mothers and Babies in South London.

Mary Breckinridge had a unique enabling plan. The nurses who would be riding forth to reach the isolated cabins where a baby was expected would be assisted by the idealistic daughters of rich parents who had given their children horses to play with throughout their childhood. They would be called "couriers." These young women riders - and I was surely one of them - could be counted on to lose their hearts in Kentucky, although not their senses. Only a few would become midwives. That would require professional training abroad, since there was no midwifery school in the United States at the time, but all would return home to become ardent fund-raisers for the Frontier Nursing Service. I believe the first midwifery school in our country was developed at the little hospital in Hyden, Kentucky, its outlines worked out by these brave nurses, one doctor on call, and Mary Breckinridge.

To my amusement, I had to take a riding-test at a huge building to which I had paid little attention heretofore; it may have been an armory or the Hippodrome where circuses were held. I directed my unknown steed to walk, trot, canter, gallup around a sawdust track. Okay? Test passed! Not long after, I arrived by Greyhound bus - a new ride, for me - wearing my jodhpurs. The bus driver knew to stop at an unmarked lane where a courier was waiting with an extra horse. On the way to the Frontier Nursing Center at Wendover, the courier filled my mind with lyrical names, some of which I still remember. Greasy Creek Mines. The six out-post nurses' homes and clinics at Beech Fork, Redbird, Pine Mountain, Bob Fork, Wooten, Bowling...No! That was the name of a local family which gave much help. I tried to remember that the very first nurse-midwife had been Ellen Halshall. Now I would meet (Gladys) Peacock and (Mary B.) Willeford. Kate Ireland was a tireless organizer beyond the mountains and so was Helen Stone, and I would be lucky if I got to ride out with Margaret from London, with the long legs of an easy rider and competent hands for catching babies. As I made friends with my new horse I strained to hear the information the courier tossed back at me over her shoulder.

It was at the Frontier Nursing Service that I had the opportunity to use my originally playful familiarity with horses - although I had to learn about the "running walk," a gait that would not break bottles in the saddlebags. I did not ultimately become a midwife or a groom, but observing rural poverty showed me that there were conditions in the land crying out for more fundamental change than this most imaginative charity could effect, God bless it! Bending over the hooves of horses bleeding with cuts from the iced-over streams they had to ford, riding out on nights so dark one could not see the horse's ears, making tea to the stringent specifications of English heroines, leading a little white mule loaded with photographic equipment that would help Marvin Breckinridge tell the F.N.S. Kentucky story to the world - these roles felt downwardly mobile, ruggedly so, except that - as Rita Mae Brown asserts - there would be a time when I could choose to go home.

Years later, my daughter Holly wrote "Mountain Song," which she has sung the world over. Her introduction tells about a Kentucky woman who refused to move when the coal companies came to strip-mine the land to which she had clung precariously all her life. "The local police carried the old woman off to jail, but the part of the story that inspired a song is that she did not go willingly!" The audience cheers when Holly adds dryly, as in a news report, "The old woman's family came down out of the mountains with their hog rifles and liberated her from jail." These were the people served by the Frontier Nursing Service.

Riding up hill and down dale, I had long conversations with Bland Morrow, the social worker who escorted country children to eye and ear specialists in Louisville: Mrs. Breckinridge had recruited a caring and professional network beyond the mountains. Still, I never heard it asked, "Why are these stalwart people among the forgotten poor?" I'm sure there was talk, but no political issues were raised at the Frontier Nursing Service - not within my hearing, one of the couriers. If there had been, metropolitan support might well have plummeted - helping the rural poor makes wealthy urban people feel good, challenging economic inequality makes the contributor nervous. I had no answers, myself, at the time, but I yearned to be one with the Kentucky hill people, rather than a delegate of their manifestly beloved colonizers. I have heard that one courier did move to a cabin high on a steep slope in Hazard County. Was this *downward mobility* for her?

Another adventure away from my idyllic college campus in Vermont was a visit to the Catholic Worker on Mott Street in the Bowery of New York City. I had been introduced to Catholicism by the professor of French literature, Wallace Fowlie, aforementioned. Through his teaching, I had learned to revere the name of Jacques Maritain, a living philosopher. The cathedral-like architecture of his thought with all its detail elicited my astonishment. Fascinated, I sat with black-pinafored students in a Paris school room as Maritain discussed such thorny questions as, "If God is all-powerful, can he make something that has been, not have been?" Following my tendency to seek synthesis, on returning to New York I attended lectures on the Catholic trade union movement, which gave me the opportunity to observe the way-

way-with-life of a tough-minded parish priest-of-the-people. I have always been moved by the appearance of religion coming down to earth.

I spent time at Dorothy Day's Hospitality House in the Bowery, doing menial tasks reverently. I helped get out mailings, but I was not yet ready to engage in discourse with this noble woman who had chosen a hands-on relationship with poverty. She took up residence among those who were totally down and out, gathered food, fed whoever came around hungry, and even housed the homeless...who in those days were a relative few compared with the homeless given rise to by the Reagan era. I don't know what limits Dorothy Day had. How did she decide who filled her few spare rooms and who ate at her table? I ran into my own limits when I invited the whole Mott Street staff and volunteers uptown to my house for dinner. It almost worked, but this fragile circle was shattered by one man who brought a bottle and tried to enliven the party by provoking a fight. I was unprepared to know how to manage such a raucous incident. My Catholic Worker friends were sorry, but probably felt, justly, it was a part of my initiation into a world with which they coped every day. I chaperoned some Greek children to the Catholic Worker farm in Easton, Pennsylvania, and learned what it was like to be hungry most of the time. The children had a spare but adequate diet, but they did not find much to do in the country; they could hardly wait to get back to their families living under the shadow of the Seventh Avenue El. At Mott Street, I met a dynamic character by the name of Peter Maurin. He had written a little book, *The Green Thumb Revolution*. It sounded good to me. Peter was a vagabond, talking, moving on. The title of his work stayed with me. I become alert when there is a plan for putting power where land is tilled by those who want to feed themselves.

It was on one of my rides downtown to Mott Street on The Elevated that I decided to shelve my first name of Prudence, and take down my middle name, Anne. Changing one's name is a profoundly unsettling act. However, since no one knew me at the Catholic Worker or called me Prudy, I would not be losing much. I would not have to explain that I was trying to comprehend the concept of an unalterable good and evil which only God could inspire or forgive. I would not have to explain that I was on a spiritual excursion away from Protestantism and the promise it held out for improving one's Eden-damaged soul through one's earthly behavior. *Domine non sum dignus ut intra sub tectum meum...sed tanto dic verbum et sonabitur anima mea*. Lest there be any doubt, I bear witness that the Second Avenue El, rollicking along at the level of second story windows, is an excellent vehicle for major thoughts. Women lean out of windows, pin laundry to movable cords attached to the neighboring tenement ladders, and call directions to the future generation playing in the traffic of the street below. The summer heat is invasive - unlike California where there are a few degrees of cool in every shade. Maybe someone would turn on a water hydrant. Who was entrusted with this decision? As the El thunders by, a tiny flash of red is a geranium in a pot on the fire escape. By the time I disembarked at the end of the line, my name was Anne. Of all people, it was Ruth who made the change unfailingly. She never called me anything but Anne again; she understood naming.

After my junior year in college, I took a bicycle trip to Austria with my sister and a friend, Alice Hutchins. We were in search of the experience of *gemütlichkeit*, and found a facsimile of it at the beer halls, linking arms with German and American boys in lederhosen, sitting at long, well-worn wooden tables, singing "Lili Marlene." It grieved me later to learn that this song - and no wonder - both rousing and nostalgic, was taken over by the Hitler youth. It was 1936. Hitler's power was growing in Germany; some people in the United States thought the man with the Charlie Chaplin mustache and the egomaniacal "Heil Hitler!" had law and order on his side. They said he got the trains running on time. Ruth and Alice and I stayed in Munich at the home of a lady who seemed to have belonged to the former aristocracy, but was now taking in selected boarders. She had grown sons who came to dinner, one presiding at each end of her table. I cringe as I remember my lack of political sensitivity, but our ignorance was perhaps reassuring to our hostess. The Rome-Berlin axis was imminent. Madam von Daubeneck would not have enjoyed a discussion with girlish visitors from an America that had seemed obsessed with staying neutral - to her it might have been dangerous, even fatal. Klaus gave me a ride around Munich on the back of his motorbike - I cannot remember why because there was a deep reserve in the household. That I can write so little is a measure both of my limited prowess in the German language and a sort of American innocence - or perhaps carelessness - in retrospect unforgivable. Now I understand that America does business with and puts into power these dictators - Hitler, Tojo, Mussolini, Noriega, Hussein - whom later it overthrows, and at great profit. Our people never seem to comprehend the dynamic of war business - and sacrifice so much for "the American values." They are told they can defend murder with dying.

After a week in Munich, we bought dirndls and wheels. There were many groups of marching youth on the road looking sturdy and healthy and motivated. We felt our own muscles strengthening. We stopped at little roadside pubs; no one of us drank beer - we had planned to learn in steinland, but we were spared by the discovery of *apfelsaft*. One night we stayed in a loft - the only lodging we could find in Rosenheim at nightfall because a military contingent was also in town. With some concern, we listened while heavy boots pounded the stairs below; we hoped our girlish presence would not give the wrong message to the hearty soldiers. By day, our pedaling took us through many lovely towns and farmland. We pushed our bikes up steep hills and had long, sweeping rides down the foothills of the Austrian Alps. Later, in Holland, we would discover that the contrasts of mountain biking were less tiring and more exhilarating than the evenness of flatland, where there was no rest; it seemed a parable. On the road with German youth, we felt our heritage in a zest for life, a freedom of the road. The names of Innsbruck and Garmisch-Partenkirchen still cling to my mind. We attended a performance of Jederman on a stage in Salzburg. The day before we left Munich, Ruth and I, coming along different streets - ran our bikes smack into each other - an almost impossibly unlikely miscalculation that threatened our lifelong association. We picked up our selves and our bikes and rode in silence, except for the click, click, click of a bent spoke. Reconciliation arrived without words.

When our idyllic journey was over, we took trains to separate destinations. Ruth went to Berlin to visit a friend, Adelaide Frick, who had been admitted to courses at a German medical school - having failed to be accepted at home as a serious applicant; even her own father found her goals inappropriate for a wealthy woman. In Berlin, Ruth experienced a gigantic rally and the sound of thousands calling out, "Heil Hitler!" Friendship took me to Frankfort, where Priscilla Crowell was part of student life at the university. She had found a room in the home of a Jewish family; none of her German college mates would come for her there. Such overt anti-semitism was a shock to me. I was finally beginning to see - but why did I not come home to the land of the free and the home of the brave and go screaming down the middle of the street decrying the deadly poison of racism. If I had, my soul might have been prepared to decry the racism against Native Americans, against Black Americans, against Japanese Americans, against Chinese Americans, against Jewish Americans, against Latin Americans, against Arab Americans! Do the weaknesses in our societal building await an earthquake!

A short time ago - 1990 in Tiburon, California - I attended a lecture entitled "Rescuers," given by Professor Hunecke of the University of California, a man who had tried to ascertain which qualities or experiences were held in common by those who stood out against Hitler, at great risk, even offering asylum to his victims. Hunecke's evidence affirmed three, but one has knocked the others from my memory: all the persons he interviewed spoke of a mother who taught them to do right! Dr. Hunecke interviewed thousands of people. I hope he will publish these legends of the brave - fearful, anonymous sometimes, always undaunted - and I hope they will be included in bibliographies for parenting. If his analysis is correct, then I must have done something right. All my children are outspoken in decrying racism. They are way ahead of me; they were not raised racist.

CHAPTER SEVEN

One Post-Graduate

I graduated from Bennington College one spring day in 1937. My classmates and I made up the second matriculating class; I pause to confirm my use of the word; it means enrolled, but I hear derivatively, matrix - so, coming from a womb. Bennington was indeed a birthplace for me. Now, I wanted to find a job. I wanted to be paid for work; a paycheck would be a talisman. While pursuing a master's degree in education at Columbia University, I was hired at the Professional Children's School on Broadway. I taught all subjects to the fifth grade including, I confess, French. In retrospect, I can only hope that my considerable energy and good humor made up for what I lacked in pedagogical practice; some would doubt this, but I never did allow myself to be less than two pages ahead of my students in the geography book. The school principal, Mrs. Nesbitt, was graciously supportive, but even she had misgivings when she entered the classroom during an enactment of Vachel Lindsay's poem, *The Congo*. I was trying out choral reading as it had been discussed at Columbia's Teachers' College. With my theater-oriented little students, it had gotten out of hand, uproariously. "*Then I saw the Congo, creeping through the black, cutting through the jungle with a golden track.*" As I reread this whole poem, I cannot imagine which other verses I might have deemed suitable. As a teacher of science and mathematics, my shortcomings were not anywhere near as forgivable.

The children in my classroom were all actors and models. This worked to my advantage from the point of view of discipline: School felt like time off in their perspective. This is not to suggest that they did not want to act. Doesn't everyone? They loved their jobs. After two years, it was I who felt deprived. I went to Henry Simon, an engaging poet/pedagogue holding forth at the campus on Morningside. "Please, direct me to a job where I can learn more about the real world. All my pupils carry union cards!" He heard me out and with his enigmatic smile responded, "Why don't you go to Commonwealth College?" Why not? The name was right. Soon I was on my way to Arkansas.

The goal of the school was to teach useful skills to southern organizers. I arrived with the idea that, after all my costly education, I might have something to offer. Quickly I revised that hope. I took classes in labor history and the value of the theater arts in the dissemination of political truths - a seminar conducted by Ruth Deacon. An assortment of activists and saints were learning how to write and use little skits and stand-up comedy and poetry to make points that had something to do with life and death - if one was organizing in Mena, Arkansas, in 1939.

I learned how to milk a cow, and I learned to make brown gravy by burning the flour ever so slightly in the pan. I learned what it is like when a government hangs a padlock on the library door. I learned what it is like to run out of food before you run out of courage. I went home to New York, cashed out my savings account with Grace Bank and returned to share it with Commonwealth College. Why did I have to take that long train ride; it is an enormous symptom of disaffection, to mistrust the postman!

The school stood accused. There would be a trial. I cannot pinpoint the charges, but I will never forget the brooding quiet with a patina of violence around the courthouse that hot, summer day. I was not privy to the councils of school leadership, but I was disappointed when it was decided to ask for a change of venue. I had looked forward to the drama of confronting injustice with innocence in a testimonial setting. I was prepared to testify, I'm not sure what to! Wiser southerners among us recognized a lynch mood growing since one single time a black colleague stayed overnight at the campus. While the objectives of the college did not include the founding of an interracial community in Arkansas, there was no use in having a school if no black person could be welcomed. Commonwealth College was dedicated to teaching practical democracy and the arts of change. However, the school administration did not want to be outmaneuvered in a southern courtroom, expensively. To my disappointment, they called retreat.

I rode north with Ed, a tall and quiet member of the sailors' union; Dan Garrison, a writer whose heart was big but did not have long to beat; and Ruth Deacon, dedicated director of The New Theatre of Philadelphia. For some years, The New Theatre had been producing plays of creative social purpose. Clifford Odets's *Waiting for Lefty* had been one of their hits, and Marc Blitzstein's wonderful musicals, *No for an Answer* and *Cradle Will Rock*. In all my theater-going years I had never known plays like these. It was integral to the concept of The New Theatre that there would be few, if any, professional actors. Cast members would be playing themselves. I remember a little fellow, Harry Goloff, who had been a member of the Abraham Lincoln Brigade, composed of volunteers from many countries, enlisting to defend the Republic and democracy in the Spanish Civil War. He explained that it was not so much a civil war as a rebellion by Francisco Franco, the first dictator to cast the shadow of fascism across Europe. Harry Goloff played a soldier in plays at the New Theatre. I longed to be in these plays and skits, but who was I, that I could play myself? No one seemed to know. No one offered me a role. I answered the phone, cleaned the bathrooms, swept out the theater - and almost burned it down while disposing of trash in the alley. I strolled hand in hand through the Jewish ghetto of Philadelphia with Aaron Spiegel, a young actor with a shock of black hair that fell over his eyes, who memorized every word and tune. He confided in me that his parents would be furious if they knew he was out with a goy! Stunned, I learned from his language; I had thought prejudice was a one-way street only gentiles had to travel.

World War II was upon us. I spent hours in The New Theatre script library looking for relevant plays, and found none. I had never believed in war as a way of solving disputes. There would be volumes of recorded talk after the fighting; why not talk before the able-bodied youth of both sides had to kill or die? In my pacifism, I was always drawing a parallel from my childhood with a twin - neighbor or rival, living in the closest proximity, we early on knew there was nothing to do but to be the best of friends. I saw the countries of the world as similarly positioned. Further, I knew that "the Allies," or perhaps only their corporations, but surely their anti-semites - had participated in the creation of Hitler, hoping his armies would hold at bay what they saw as threatening in the Russian Revolution. I turned my back. I said, "Thou shalt not kill." I was friends with conscientious objectors.

And then I knew that I must take part in defeating our monster. Not to do so would be tantamount to removing myself from the significant expiation - from the throbbing heart, the tormented mind, the soaring spirit, and, above all, the denouncing of racism. I visited a friend at a camp for "conscientious objectors." It was pleasant enough, in no way embattled; he had been put out to pasture! I returned to the house I was sharing with Herb and Ray Hoffman. They didn't ask about my day; it was my soul they were waiting to hear about; they were listening for the sound of my Aryan righteousness, my proper and effective fury, my Viking rage. It became impossible to cling to the purity of pacifism. I was beginning to accept an inconsistency, a willingness to compromise a key element of religious faith. A still, small voice was being overwhelmed by the roar of history and an uncommon sense of being needed. Nevertheless, I hesitated. I just could not imagine enlisting in the Army! Indubitably, there was a class element in this - I had never danced with, or shaken hands with, or met an enlisted warrior...except for Harry Goloff! I did not socialize with soldiers or policemen.

By chance, I was sent to represent The New Theatre at a meeting of cultural organizations seeking to define their roles in anti-fascism. Among them was a spokesperson for the German-Americans in Philadelphia who did not want to be sidelined or persecuted; after all, it was they who were the most experienced anti-Nazis! When his voice came from the back of the room, it was as if my German heritage, desecrated by Hitler's crimes, had been returned to me, battered but intact, entering the lists. After the meeting, I had coffee with him, and found a machinist with strong roots in the progressive labor movement. He suggested that I join the *industrial* army. Relieved, I signed up for classes where I learned about drill presses, lathes, planers and micrometers...and that there really was a use for the logarithms that I had contended with at Chapin School.

I fell in love with this working man - vibrant, competent, politically cognitive. I felt a passion that drew from every facet of my being. For too long I refused to ask whether he was free to return that love. I will not say he deceived me; how could I wish to tarnish the most integrating love of my life! I deceived myself. Even after I knew, I could not get myself to the station. Finally, finally I took a train to the farthest place on the map the tracks could go, away from my sin. For three days and four nights I perched on my suitcase in the plunging, swaying railway coach, a bunch of red roses limp in my arms, tears streaming down my cheeks unnoticed by wartime travelers, mostly soldiers, en route to the West Coast with grievous partings of their own to dwell upon. Joe, farewell!

I did not fully realize in this moment that I was putting three thousand miles between my life and that of my twin. I knew nothing of California. Literally, I drew straws between the major cities...San Diego, Santa Cruz, San Francisco...I arrived in Los Angeles without a single name to call! At that moment, Ruth was riding in a bus with other navy wives to meet their sailors shipping out on the Atlantic to torpedo German submarines, or be torpedoed.

The aircraft companies of sunny Southern California, its weather amenable to year-round manufacture, were hiring everybody, stockpiling personnel in anticipation of huge contracts if the war went on. I found a room in a small downtown hotel and went in search of the employment agency, which directed me to North American Aviation in Inglewood, where Douglas Aviation was also being built on the sandy coastal flats. With many of the skilled men drafted into the armed services, jobs were broken down into simpler tasks, for which the formerly excluded women, minorities, and older people eagerly applied. For my part, I refused jobs in management; I wanted manual work that would be under the jurisdiction of the union; I wanted to be downwardly mobile with a UAW-CIO button on my overalls. Suspicion of me arose because of the extensive education that appeared on my work summary; one was required under oath to list every occupation for the past ten years; there was fear of saboteurs. As I filled out the application I felt guilty...why? Because of my radical past? Because of my class? I was terrified that I would be disqualified from participating in the world's duel on behalf of truth. In point of fact, my ideas were never more "radical" than the Declaration of Independence, the Bill of Rights, the Ten Commandments, and the Beatitudes, literally understood. Fortunately, negative evidence in my resume was lost in the sea of paperwork and I was hired. I donned a pair of bib overalls, a flannel shirt, and a large identification badge. With lunch box and toolbox I showed up at the factory gate.

What an astonishing scene was the huge hangar at dawn, with all variety of the human species siphoned through the narrow security entrance where each worker must open toolbox and lunch box for inspection. The word, inspection, had a different meaning inside, where hundreds of people were hired to inspect the work for flaws. The women, wearing slacks or coveralls - more remarkable than it would be today - and bandannas, because there had been a scalping accident in the drill section, strode to their places by the great silver skeletons of airships in formative stages. In some areas of the hangar the noise was deafening as women wielded rivet guns, sewing together the sheets of metal that would become wings or nose cones. My first job was classified Electrician One. I crawled up into the nacelle and, lying on my stomach, tidied up the bunches of wires loosely threaded through the hull. I tied them down with a fine waxy cord and a dab of red lacquer to hold the knot. Done! Next bomber. I had expensive tools to keep track of as the line moved inexorably out the door, out toward the sky, out to the war. Until I learned never to put one down, every single week I lost a pair of long-nosed pliers or dikes, which the cutters were called. Of course they were "recycled" back into the war effort.

By wandering where the little beach houses met the blue Pacific, I found a spare and bare room much to my liking. The sand strewn with gobs of oil from tankers was right at my door. So were the magnificent sunsets over the ocean. There were a number of small towns on the steep incline to the shore; mine was Manhattan Beach, its name underlining my expatriation. I climbed to catch a bus to my job, which was clocked at ten hours a day, six days a week, and stumbled gratefully downhill to my place when the day was done.

61

It was virtually impossible for a foreman to find something for the eager women workers to do all that time - 10 hours a day, six days a week. We were so many...and some, who had husbands overseas, were outraged by idleness. "How would my hubby feel to see me sitting around!" I cannot describe the boredom of starting the day with nothing to do, and nine-and-a-half hours to go till the whistle. "Go hide!" the foreman said. "Hide?" "Yes, I said, hide! Pick up a piece of paper and carry it around the plant! Get outa sight, now!" But there were other days when I earned my salt and felt deeply satisfied to be part of the extraordinarily egalitarian effort to put wings under the defense of democracy. It is hard to remember now that there were times when it was not a foregone conclusion that we would win. Recently, I found a letter I had written to Ruth expressing my day's frustration.

Dear Ruth,

My work is most exasperating, in spite of being so picturesque. Specifically, it's all trouble. The day starts with shortages - everything incomplete. One waits. Then one is handed a bunch of "spaghetti" yards long to install. There are holes to drill, clamps and buttons to find, rubber grommets to be wedged into holes...and when the day is done, you must leave it to someone else. And also, everyone is on top of you. Imagine a space half the size of your bathroom...with no floor in it, just a ledge...and six or eight people with yards of electric wire, hand electric drills trailing up the ladder. Others with pipes and air-hoses and leather cushions to be installed (Not to sit on!) And yourself loaded down with tools you might need, and three more people trying to get up with more junk. And a few others just "hiding" because there's nothing to do right now, but they have to look like they're working. You find yourself talking to yourself. "Look, Prudy, what do you care! Don't get neurotic trying to accomplish something. You get paid if ten

62

people are climbing all over you just as much as if you were alone with room to work well. Take it easy. Work if you can, but take it easy! *It's all in your ten hours.*"

I recall my elation in deciding that I was now a member of the working class in a society at risk - the society that had been a beacon of hope to "the huddled masses yearning to breathe free." Timidly I entered the union hall after work. Local 887 was organizing from a small building across the highway from the plant; it was uphill work, I was told, because an unsuccessful strike before the war years had left disillusionment in its wake. Besides, in the workforce were many who did not plan to be there once the men came home. But some men would not come home, and some women would not go home, now that the plant doors had been opened to them. Job descriptions and pay scales were being demanded, and they were changing so rapidly that it was hard for a union shop steward to argue "a grievance"; there were few precedents. Patriotism seemed to require that all "beefs" be endured rather than negotiated. Before the war, a master machinist made something, rather than simply performing a task. By 1944, much of factory work had been transformed into a million little chores. Still, my concept of patriotism rested on a trust, not in the upper echelons of corporate management, but in those who, to get ahead, must bring all others up with them; I had learned this at the New School for Social Research in New York City; it was well worth the price of all my courses. I joined the union and was one of disappointingly few women attending meetings. I had looked forward to hearing the United Auto and Aircraft Workers of America version of Mother Jones, who exhorted the mineworkers many years ago; she was not there. I now know that it is very difficult for women to be there when they have children and households to keep together, especially after working a ten-hour day while their men are off to war. Women have not been taught ambition from childhood, but rather homemaking or survival - most women who worked away from the home, did so because they had to.

After some months at North American Aviation, I was chosen by the union to be the women's representative to a newly constituted labor-management committee, instructed to find ways to maximize the war effort and do something about the costly war production problem of plant turn-over. Of course, it wasn't the plant that was turning over. The Union wrote to The Labor-Management Committee, "...the experience of seeing hundreds of aircraft workers come through our gates, only to leave a few months later, leads us to propose that The Labor Management Committee can most fruitfully consider the problem of man-power shortage as one of personnel turn over."

The union then pointed out that the UAW/CIO had a program, publically known, based on the causes of instability as they saw them daily: Health, Housing, Transportation, Cost of Living, Wages, Child Care, Morale, and so on. Local 887 ended its call with the following paragraph.

> If we succeed at all, it shall not be said that North American Aviation, builders of two of the proudest ships of the aircraft fleet of the United States, remained among the first on the dishonor list of priority for man-power shortage, because it was unable to enlist the support and capture the imagination of its workers - and that the Labor Management Committee did nothing about it.

Such was the earnestness of Local 887, UAW/CIO in September, 1943.

If it had not been for Hitler, Franco, Mussolini, and Tojo, I would have had nothing to do with a labor-management committee because I understood the union movement as essentially adversarial in its finest moments. It is not a tool for "getting along," but for changing the shameful ratios of rich to poor. There were "suggestion boxes" to be filled by workers' creativity - a war-time gift to management.

I first saw Russell Near from the window of a B-57. He was driving the train of little cars that delivered machined parts to every area of the factory. He was a dictionary, identifying every screw and lock-washer a worker on the assembly line might need. What a good job for a union organizer! He got around. Management sensed his engaging presence and offered him higher

64

paid executive jobs that would move him off the floor; he would have none of them. Later, when we were both members of a committee to review the union contract with North American Aviation, I had the chance to observe his affable but uncompromising philosophy of labor relations. I was pleased when he consulted me about women's working conditions; I had to learn about them, myself. We discovered that what was physiologically hurtful for women - such as standing long hours on concrete - was not good for men either.

Once upon a time, Russell and I were married. Even in the kindliness of our fortieth anniversary, we never spoke of love at first sight. The facts were that I had no time in my schedule to date and no room in my self-image for getting pregnant out of wedlock; Russell's schedule included union work at two other aircraft plants and membership in the CIO Council. So we got married. I don't know why he married me...to the great surprise of associates who considered him "the playboy of the western world." I do know why I married him; he was handsome and intelligent and radical and had strong roots in American history. If anyone wanted to call him a "Comm-u-nist," they'd have to admit he was an indigenous one. Sometimes I think I decided that I wanted to marry Russell when I saw his parents, brushed with the winds of North Dakota, still together and settled now in California.

There was no time for the wedding to be a grand scene. Come to think of it, I had no one to invite. I did not make friends in the aircraft factory. After ten hours together on the line, we women were ready to part. My family had not disowned me - the welcome mat was still out at East Coast doorways - but there were big signs in every place of travel, supporting the war effort: IS THIS TRIP REALLY NECESSARY? No. Of course not! I had "given myself away" from my family's dominion years earlier. No need to do it twice. Still, married we were in a little ceremony in Russell's parents' parlor. The Presbyterian minister had a harder time than we, carrying off the prenuptial conference required; we were 27 and 36. At the wedding I remember Russell's brother Perry wearing a white Navy suit, and his brother Lloyd in tan civvies - an inventor whose genius was being exploited by an employer in the war industry - or so his father thought. We all had to wait for

Fred Near to get home from his job at Douglas Aviation, by trolley; he was seventy years old and pushing a wide broom across the factory floor...for the war effort. A banker in earlier days, in Beach, North Dakota, his goodwill was touching, and evidence of a democratization that happens in the pursuance of a "just" war, if one can entertain this concept through the moment when all arms are laid down. (I see a tendency on the part of leaders to take care of a little extra business for themselves while they're at it.)

Edna Near was not at all sure what her son was getting into, marrying a New Yorker in overalls; when we first met, I was lying flat on her floor with a sciatic nerve flare-up. I told her that I was taken by her son's sweet voice when he grabbed the mike at a union dance. "What were you singing, Russell?" she asked with mock concern. "'Come Along and Be My Sweetie Pie,'" he claimed. "Oh?" I told Mrs. Near that it was "The Ballad of Joe Hill." "You must sing that for me, sometime, Russell," she said.

> I dreamed I saw Joe Hill last night
> Alive as you and me
> Said I, "But Joe,
> You're ten years dead!"
> "I never died," said he.
> "I never died," said he.

Mrs. Near had cooked a fine pot roast, North Dakota style, in a deep pan filled with carrots and onions and potatoes. We spoke the name of Lowell, another son/brother who was with General Patton in Africa. The minister led us through the marriage language as written; we made no "corrections". Quaint as it seemed in 1942, we made all the promises and never broke a one, honoring and obeying till death did us part. On our wedding night, as we undressed, I remember Russell casually saying that he had a bad leg left over from childhood polio. Of course I knew he had a bad leg. I had been watching his lilting limp since I first spotted him. No more was said. Waking up in our attic bedroom the first morning of our married life, I saw Russell's work boots, one skewed, lined up on the floor. I had never known a man with shoes like that. Downwardly mobile? You bet! My eyes fell upon the flowery little book the minister had left with us; it would provide the dates to prove our first born quite "legitimate" when she showed up a year later. We named her Timothy after the grasses that blew on the plains of her father's native North Dakota. When Russ and I came downstairs at dawn to go to work, Mrs. Near had packed both our lunch boxes with sandwiches of butter on salt-rising bread.

When World War II was brought to a dumbfounding conclusion with the dropping of the unimaginable atomic bomb, we could not have dreamed there were more wars to follow. War was over. It would be an anachronism, unthinkable. The "reds" who had done yeoman work in the wartime plant, including union work, were no longer welcome in Walter Reuther's plan. (Has the day arrived when I need to say who Walter Reuther was? He was president of United Auto and Aircraft Workers of America, but he was not immune to the McCarthy scourge of "red-baiting," with all its career destroying folly.) Russell lost his union job without which he no longer had seniority, a perk contractually accorded union officers. North American Aviation could fire him. They did.

We used a bequest from my grandfather and our War Bonds for a down payment on a house for Russell's parents, and redid the garage for us. In filial enthusiasm, we bought a place too large for Fred Near to care for, in the way he had demanded of others - and now, of himself. It was a sweet place...with fruit trees to be pruned and cultivated. Then Russell, somewhat disoriented by his sudden unemployment, got together with a friend, Preston Tuttle, to make a toy train on which a child could ride down a thirty-foot track assembled from surplus aircraft parts. It was a beauty, as was his partnership with the designer, but after their production costs were doubled by the distributor and doubled again by Schwartz & Co. Toys, it became apparent that only very rich kids would get to ride this train. Preston found his way back to academia, and Russell was on the loose again. Time for my husband to meet my family, and they him. We bought an old but cruise-appropriate Lincoln Continental and drove across the continent. Russell loved acquainting himself with the Lincoln's mechanical personality. While we were visiting in Pennsylvania, we received word that Russell's father had had a heart attack. As we prepared to return immediately, another message followed.

Russell's mother had died - perhaps pushing her limits as she cared for Fred. We abandoned our car and took a plane. Miserable, crowded knee to knee, we talked about the relationship three-year-old Timi had with her grandfather - mutual adoration, almost *forsaking all others*. We comforted ourselves by anticipating the joy her smile could bring to him, but when she saw him lying in bed and ashen gray, she was afraid; this was not her rambunctious Grandpa Fred. And his attention to dying would allow no room for a child. Russell held him tight as he seemed to fight his way out of the world, bleak without his wife.

Sorrow does not necessarily bring people closer. This was a critical time in my relationship with Russell; I seemed to be allowed no place in the family loss, although in some genealogic way I had married Russell because of seeing his parents in him. I had to swallow my sobs at both funerals; I grieved in secret and Russell was left alone to take up his role as one of the primary generation. We never spoke of this, never found each other's arms, we just went on. It could have been a time for Russell to find his way back to the union movement and the fervor we had shared. He didn't appear to be doing anything, day after day. It was I who became worried, out of sight of land, out of sight of the defining shores of paid occupation. Idly I dusted the Near house; idly with Timi I leafed through family albums. I saw a farm in North Dakota, men operating a combine, four little boys atop an old dray horse, the cylinder of a granary dwarfing a two-story wooden house, Russell's grandfather - a boy during the Civil War - now, swinging a milk bucket, his mother hanging out sheets, horizontal in the wind. "We could go ranching," I said to Russ.

His face lit up. "Wanna be a cowgirl, Tim?"

"Cow-girp?"

"Cow-girps and cowboys - we might give it a try."

I never believed Russ would actually do this. People fantasize about going to the country; it's a way of knocking their day at the office. Not Russ! He bought a spanking new, forest green pick-up truck with a canvas caravan top over the bed, and we headed away in search of good work - unrelated to any part of war or its detritus. "Joe Hill" was left behind.

Russell and I were married at his parents' home.

Lowell, Russell's brother, was a soldier with General Patton.

Local 887's delegation to the CIO convention. A few of us were women.

Russell's parents, Fred and Edna Near, take their boys out for a drive in Beech, North Dakota.

Charles Augustus Near, at his home in North Dakota and with his Civil War compatriots.

Fred's mother, Sarah Augusta Perry Near, and Edna's mother, Maria Coleman Peek, with their first grandchild: which one was the socialist?

CHAPTER EIGHT

Potter Valley Ranch

After driving all over the state of California, sleeping on beaches or in the truck bed, we found a rugged, hill-land property in Potter Valley - eighteen hundred acres, within our means. It looked like a real ranch. We could have made a better livelihood growing pears, but no one showed us an orchard for sale. Perhaps we did not dress like serious buyers. (Today, if a man has an earring in his ear, brokers will show him 10,000 acres! Marijuana is a major agricultural crop in Mendocino County. Actually, it doesn't take 10,000 acres to grow pot - a few acres will produce a huge yield when carefully hidden from the roving helicopters of the "narcs.") It was winter, the season when there is a show of green on Mendocino County slopes - idyllic, until it turns brown in late May. We discovered that it would take at least ten acres of our scrubby soil to grow the food for one cow, and she would have to pick it herself; it would never get high enough for a sickle. Nor were we then aware of the political implications of growing cattle to supply protein. So much water, turf, fresh bunch-grass, and winnowed grain to produce one pound of hamburger! It seemed just fine to us to be plowing our war bonds into the good earth. We did not have the concepts for self-criticism as farmers, and we had not yet heard of tofu or soybeans as a viable and cheaper protein source than meat for feeding the world. Together Russell and I set out to learn the multiple skills of animal husbandry and land stewardship in Northern California, but it was not long - with all the blossoming and aborning, dehorning and castrating and branding - before Russ became the rancher among men, and I, learning to make wild blackberry jam and venison stew, the rancher's wife among a brood of children with all outdoors as their play yard.

71

Let me step back a moment, to beginnings. Russell and his brother had gone on ahead to accept the Potter Valley property - both the land and the cattle that came with it; they had been warned to "count heads." Timi and I had stayed behind to close down our southern California home forever. This geography was hard on both of us. When I didn't hear from Russ for three whole days, I allowed anger into the phone call he had gone to some pains to make; of course there was no phone near by. Russ mailed postcards.

"The delay is killing me too. Being away from you for two weeks is just plain hell for me. I might as well be without food and water. My heart is starved for the sight of you too. Holy Christ, how did I get along before?"

Another post card was no more reserved. "Yesterday somebody let our cattle out - probably hunters. I saddled old Snaps and brought them in. It is going to be wonderful to get together here on the hillside, drink it in together. Love to all and a double header for you and my Tim." Does the post man read the postcards?

"Tiny Tim, someday your mommy will take you to find daddy - soon - and we'll all be happy here on our ranch. Believe me darling, it won't be too long. We're putting in temporary stanchions for uncle Lloyd's milk cows, building feed racks, and developing a watering hole near the barn. Tell mommy hugs, Daddy"

Another postcard was scribbled in pencil. "Yesterday we helped bob the tails of 59 wild critters. We had a whale of a time wrestling calves, cussing, sweating, sliding in the shit. Only one got away, taking off over the fence and into the hills like a deer. Darling, we're in this business up to our belt buckles. Only your in the wrong territory. Could you and Tim come now? Think about it."

We were met at the train station in Alameda by two ruddy fellows. Russ had put away his hangar look, the pallor that comes with working under fluorescent lights. He wore the mark of the sun. As Russ drove, the men talked excitedly as kids explaining a new game...the proper depth for a sturdy post-hole, the possibility of plowing level benchland for planting oats, the nutrients in soil, the best way to build a manger, how to turn a calf that could not come through the mother's pelvic bones. I thought they were showing off a bit; I was very excited.

"You should see this enormous white barn, Anne! You've never seen such a barn!"

"I won't miss it, Russ."

"Tim, guess what? The discer turned up a little girl's red shoe, all muddy," reported Lowell.

"Cockadoodle doo, my master's lost a shoe. My master's lost his fiddledy stick and..." began Timi, who was up on her nursery rhymes. She knew something big was afoot because no one was paying much attention to her. She had not expected Unkie Lolo to be with her father. He was a soldier.

The men went on talking about the merits of a round baler, which rolled up the hay and tied it with string, and of a thermos that could catapult down a mountainside and never break. To my astonishment, even with this reminder, we never stopped, not once, for coffee. I was picking up hints. I saw the landscape change from meadows to steep hills. It was not until Russ announced that we were crossing our cattle-guard that I began to wonder what I, myself, would be doing on this place. It was dusk. The peace was so absolute that a gray deer did not take fright as we passed, but went on grazing. I will be alone here with Tim, maybe a lot of the time. Russ pulled up by a little white box of a house. This is it? I was overjoyed. The kitchen was small, the biggest room. There was a table but no chairs. I hoisted myself up on a wooden drainboard and made the acquaintance of an enormous cast iron stove. I had no idea how challenging it would be to persuade it to do the cooking. Sometimes its lids would turn red with rage, other times it would smoke, moodily without warmth; sometimes it would reach biscuit browning perfection, an hour after Russ had gone back on the mountain with a handful of crackers for his lunch. I thought of my cookbook. Bake at 425° for fifteen minutes, then reduce heat to 325°. Hi, stove!

Russell and Lowell went right down to the barn - already ranchers with the right priorities. I found a box of matches and began to light a kerosene lamp. Good Adirondack memories flooded over me bringing familiarity's encouragement. Black smoke poured up the glass chimney. The wick had not been trimmed; I knew about that. I turned on a faucet and water gushed out, teaching me a lot about gravity flow. Russ had told me there were many springs - we would not have to skimp on water. I looked out the window above the sink and saw the hills hovering over us, delivering this great blessing.

I hopped down from the drainboard and walked around; it was not a long walk. I discovered two little rooms, both served by the bathroom between them. That was all. Not much housekeeping...if we cover our "things" with a tarp and leave them outside on the trailer. A washboard leaned against the wall; I ran my fingers down its rounded scrub-surfaces. In the dim light I could see a denim shirt rolled in a ball and tossed in a corner. Some things were familiar; here, as always, the floor is nearer than the laundry basket. The shirt appeared to be torn straight down the back. How does this happen? I had not learned about barbed wire, yet. Still, it would be an easy job for a sewing machine. No electricity! I fondly remembered Mrs. Near's treadle machine; it had seemed quaint to me last week. I hoped we had not left it behind.

Russ clomped in, his step heavy with the weight of a huge bucket of milk. With amazement I looked at the frothy plenitude flecked with bits of hay. He pointed to a large silver strainer on the wall and an enormous earthenware bowl. Clearly, he was demonstrating procedures that would be my job. "You wash the pail before the milk has a chance to set on it." He shrugged toward the double washtubs. "When the cream comes up - like tomorrow morning - you skim it off to go with the oatmeal." "What'll I do with all...the rest?" "I'll get you a pig." Russ was not sure what was coming off when I threw my arms around his neck. I was overcome with happiness. I had learned to milk a cow in Arkansas, and learned to ride on Long Island, and how to care for horses at the Frontier Nursing Service, and how to cook on a shoestring at the Catholic Worker farm in Pennsylvania, and how to have a baby in a cabin in Kentucky...but maybe that would not be necessary for me. I had a few of the ingredients that go into the making of a rancher's wife, but I had never had a pig. We did not get one until my niece, Hilda Bacon, visiting from Philadelphia and becoming weary at the auction sale we all attended regularly, as if it were a social club, raised her hand by mistake and found herself the owner of two little black and white pigs. She called them Hilda

Ham and Crispy Bacon after guinea pigs of her acquaintance. Crispy was a great pet, but my son, Fred, who arrived third in the line-up, and had joined the local 4-H by the time he was six, raised pigs later in a more entrepreneurial fashion. The pigs were a handy garbage-disposal unit for me, but I am told this is not legal anymore, if a pig is to be sold out of the family. The contradictions on a ranch between pets and provender are stark, but children seem to handle them better than their mothers do. I suppose because we have nurtured the child with his pet, an endearing composition. A lot of my heart went into this sometimes messy portrait, but Russ declared he would never eat any animal that had a name.

I had to deal with being alone at night. This lesson arrived soon, when Russell told me he was going to Yreka with Lowell to pick up a batch of calves he would raise on the grass and the oats from the oatfield. "Where you found the shoe?" asked Timi. "Betcha! Good-bye - only for a week." That night, to Timi's surprise, I invited her to sleep in my bed; this rarely happened. The bed was on an open porch. I lay and listened to the owls calling to each other up the hill. I heard the very distant laughter of the coyotes. I began to wonder if the butter I had churned was all right in the wooden cask until morning. I heard the cats' caterwauling. I put the sheet over my head and felt fear. Then some wisp of ancient magic all women know came to fortify my heart. I slipped out of bed, tucked the covers around Timi so she would not feel me gone, and went outside. It was a moonless night. I walked all round the house and down to the barn and along the edge of the oatfield in the smooth path that had not been plowed and around the looming rocks, so they could no way scare me. I became very calm; I was never again afraid of the dark.

"Where did you go?" murmured Timi, who had inched over to my side of the bed.

"Out into the sweet, black night."

"Me, too."

I think of the next twenty years as the trunk of my life, with the rest - before and after - as roots, branches, and leaves. Russell and I both worked hard on a place euphemistically called a "one-man ranch." However, it was not a one-man ranch in the curious pretension that a family farm is a bachelor's bailiwick.

Besides employing a wife, ours was a two-man ranch because of a friendship since childhood between brothers. Lowell and Russell had arrived on earth on dates so close - for not being twins - that one is inclined to imagine their parents' somewhat impatient post-partum love. A warrior in World War II, Lowell's job had been to write the hometown folks about their sons' exploits at the front. An old union man with the streetcar conductors, Lowell expected Russ to send him "organizing" reports while he himself enlisted to fight fascism. At the time of my story Lowell was a tendentious anceunt undergraduate at Berkeley where he was moving inexorably, if somewhat reluctantly, toward a teaching credential. Lowell used our ranch as a recreational scenario: he brought younger student friends to "ride for cattle" and discuss the political world at our long table with its stupendous view of cow country. We enjoyed the seminar.

Even more affective upon us was Lowell's meeting Jean Gowan, who was instructing a square dance party at the Grange Hall in Potter Valley. Jean was the daughter of Judd Gowan, the cattle buyer, and Grace, who wrote the Potter Valley News for the Ukiah Daily Journal. Both were archetypal; when Lowell married Jean, our immigrant family from Los Angeles was wed with the history of Mendocino County. It was not easy for Jean to find her space in such a verbally aggressive enclave; there never seemed to be a door ajar through which her quiet wisdom could enter. Still, she must have known that she was giving us locale.

Jean had two teenage sons who regarded Lowell's intrusion with justifiable suspicion, and he regarded them as a challenge premonitory of his oncoming profession. At that time, and maybe still, the primary qualification of a teacher - the *sine qua non* - was the ability to control. Bill and John were large, handsome fellows with no interest in being controlled, but time raced past all dilemmas. When the boys were off and away with distinguished careers. Lowell and Jean bought a sheep ranch in the wild country above Redwood Valley. Because of predator coyotes, the sheep came down to corrals at evening and were watched over by an extraordinary sheepdog of mixed lineage. It was here that Lowell died alone one morning as he was doing what he loved best: feeding his animals before turning them up on the hill to fend for themselves on the sparse green adorning the mountain meadows

76

of Mendocino County. Jean stayed - an impressive, colorful, endearing figure, known as both iris connoisseur and "sheep-woman."

The auxiliary richness of our cultural experience was greatly enhanced by contributions from my mother - tickets for one or another or all of us to New York, Philadelphia, London, or an overnight stay with her at the St. Francis Hotel on Union Square in "our city," San Francisco. I can still see Timi cautiously pulling out all the empty bureau drawers in the huge room and trying to use each one to hold the little things in her suitcase. I can still see my small, blue-jeaned boy practicing the art of letting all the ladies step out first from the crowded elevator. I remember Laurel worrying about what the pigeons found to eat, so high on the cornices outside the window of the hotel room. I remember the studio on Powell Street where an aging music teacher picked up a little extra money by making direct-to-disc records. Holly told him she needed one "...to send Grandma for Christmas?" "Of course," he said, adjusted his dials and sat back, releasing control. She sang all the Christmas tunes she knew and filled the remaining grooves with "Que Sera, Sera." I remember the second-story window announcing Stage Craft Studios, where Holly found a "flying jacket" so she could be Peter Pan, aloft above the stage of the Redwood Empire Fair. I remember swinging along Geary Street with Timi at Christmas when she confided in me, "I know a lot about the cattle are lowing, but I could enjoy a little more frankincense and myrrh." For many years, Laurel was too young to go on urban excursions, but she was the one to whom my mother gave a baby dachshund so that she would have someone to love, smaller and younger than herself. When she did finally get to go, and took her turn with Santa, in Macy's window, she was filled with misgivings..."I do not think I should be sitting on your lap!" I remember difficulties overcome to take Holly to see *Porgy and Bess*, and my remorse when her first introduction to the black cast included a frightening scene of gambling, murder, and rape, whereas, from my living room in Potter Valley, I had thought only of Gershwin's grand music and endearing characters. *I loves you, Porgy. Don't let him take me. Don't let him handle me and drive me mad. Those melodies! There's a boat that's leaving soon for New York.*

In spite of these romantic city journeys, enabled by my mother, our lives did not change except with the seasons. From what we earned raising calves to sell - and living where this could be done - we could not have sent our children away by train and plane or ship to see the world - not even to the inspiring East Coast family assemblies. Nonetheless, without Russell's labor out under the weather, sunup to sundown, our children would not have felt themselves to be - nor been perceived to be - "raised on a ranch." This gave them an identity defined by what their father did for a living - as I was also defined, a rancher's wife.

There came a time when we needed to expand our household space. We agonized over enlarging. In our minds, we pushed the kitchen wall out maybe five feet, the bedroom to the west, two feet, the other bedroom, four feet to allow for another child. Ruth's husband, Ed Bacon, a city planner and architect, came visiting on his way to China. It was haying time. Ed worked with the Potter Valley boys - loading hay from dawn to noon - and then quit without apology. The young men liked him, were surprised by his energy; they called him, "Morning Glory." Ed studied our house. "Forget improvements," he said. "Add one great room." The advice had inestimable consequences. The new enclosure invited people to move - as do his urban designs. Dancers found step-it-out room. Tricycles whirled around the pink stone fireplace in the center. No one, even readers, was run over or in any other way excluded. Huge window-walls with leaded panes framed mountain vistas and at night became great mirrors. I don't think it was the architect's fault that Holly, dressed in a white bunny coat and playing with Fred while I did a last pick-up before rushing out the door for Easter church, put her arm through one of the panes. Just a little blood can look terrible on a bunny coat.

I trusted my mother with the little rejoicings that it is more seemly to keep to oneself - for example, my pride in my four children, her grandchildren, after all - and my surprise in the borders they chose to cross. You do not need to renounce ambition if you adjust the direction of your pride. For example, my mother and I traded in a New Yorker's fantasy of Timothy appearing on a Broadway stage for the image of her traveling to Australia as a hand-eloquent actress/interpreter with the National Theatre of the Deaf. Unable to take part in the future, she cultivated ways of reaching it through devising accolades, this grandmother did.

Still, the journey I needed to take was away from her. It is one of life's oddest trips, unmapped, unrecognized, and proceeding along an unreliable path from class to class. The route is seldom direct and never to be trusted. My mother tried to understand, but I had to defend the integrity of my choices from her ever-ready checkbook. She had an artist's enthusiasm for the shape of workingmen's tools. She made a beautiful drawing in sepia pencil of the fence pliers Russ wore at his belt. During World War II, she had loved that I "made airplanes." She was entranced when we moved to a cattle ranch; she had the address and brand engraved on stationery (green-on-green from Tiffany's) she used while living with us; I don't believe she ever inquired as to how the brand was stuck onto the cow's hide, presumably painless as a signature, but she did not visit the corrals to hear the calves bawling. She loved the look of blue denim, but she could not resist sending her son-in-law a leather coat from Abercrombie & Fitch. With a flourish she could have written a check worth all the calves he could raise in a year of early risings, long days in the saddle, fence building, water development, and cowboy camaraderie. My mother never understood how her money endangered the very core of what she admired, including my determination to participate at a physical level in the work of the world. Russ might ask with a grin, "Whose work?" But he would agree I stretched the limits of housewife-mother, even to the top of the mountain.

My mother's daughter, it took time for me to comprehend another distinction: being hardworking ranchers did not make us farmworkers, with all the honorable connotations historically associated with that labor - including the name of Cesar Chavez - any more than sailing on the Queen Mary aligned us with Harry Bridges and the maritime union. Many years later, our daughter Holly, who grew up on a ranch but wandered far afield as a political troubadour, would introduce a song with these words, "I have just come from where mighty organizers have some endless spirit and the ability to see their future very clearly. They are called the United Farm Workers. I was taking part in an event a while ago when they arrived, one hundred and fifty strong, all on stage singing together - men, women, and children. They had faces like maps of the earth. These are the people who feed us and meanwhile are starving." No, we were not farm-workers in Potter Valley; we owned eighteen hundred acres.

Looking back at the ranch in
Potter Valley.

Russell on his appaloosa, "Blue"...and on the front porch

...raised on a ranch.

Timothy

Fred

Holly & Laurel

I'm so glad we took pictures.

Russell and Holly liked to sing together.

Timothy rode her horse to school.

Fred and Laurel supervise the evening milking.

CHAPTER NINE

Talking About Lawrance

It is past time to take a breath and talk again about my brother, Lawrance. The fraternal sense of him was always strong with me, and often in the context of our parents' opinion that the twins did everything right...and he did almost everything wrong. I think he played into this facile theorem, and I did, too. My most defeating weakness is ever still that I am too well-behaved, in a world that could benefit from a little more questioning, a lot more defiance - on everybody's part. When I pore over old albums in search of Lawrance, I see a little boy adoring his mother; my actual memories show me a growing young man who tried to be like his father. It was impossible. Popular himself, Lawrance never learned Judge's respectful way with popularity. Lawrance deserted his many friends at St. Paul's prep school, and in the Ivy Club at Princeton, as they reached out to him. He was an unpracticed soloist, unaware of his choir. And Lawrance was the one who carried forward into the next generation my mother's family strain of hypochondria; our maternal grandmother died in England seeking medical expertise while New York doctors protested that there was nothing wrong; our mother avoided the delusion by having so much that was wrong as a result of osteomyelitis. She was breakable! Ruth and I resisted this heritage to the point of stoicism, but we appreciated our brother's rueful laughter at his troubles, which were actual, serious, and finally fatal. In the meantime, Lawrance, perhaps suffering acute tenderness toward her, dreamed up ways to outrage his mother who never could refuse him anything.

Lawrance's assessment of my abilities was always extreme. He would tell people that his sister was more brilliant than they could easily imagine. This did not help me at all at the

Junior Prom. Besides, I was not flattered because I felt he had no idea of what acquired competence was all about; he did not practice anything. Lawrance did not stay long in one job, but not because he lacked the genius to succeed. He started PIC Magazine at Street & Smith, where he was at least a candidate scion of the evolving old publishing company. He left. He went upstate and bought The Independent Republican & Democrat (sic) in Goshen, New York, and then set about courting the indignation of his chosen citizenry with editorials that flagrantly violated their taste and beliefs. And this is not to imply that Lawrance was a man with a cause; he was simply replaying his childhood story.

Lawrance won the love of four fabulous women; he married and extolled each wife as the highest expression of womanhood we, his sisters, would ever be so fortunate as to encounter. My mother welcomed every single daughter-in-law to her heart, and was not inclined to dissolve her affections just because her son moved on, to Lawrance's annoyance. My brother had nine children, five of them prior to my being a mother. In my own outsize hands I can still see the shape of those larger ones with which he held each youngster. To my present shame, I never offered to babysit. Did you notice, Dorothy, Judge, Toni, Kate, John, Nick, George, Julie, Liz? Did you ever wonder what aunts are for? Since, surely, children lend stature, I must consider my lack of generosity in child care to be one aspect of my *downward mobility* - but it did not last a lifetime. I realize now how much I like them and admire their talents.

During one of our rare visits to New York, my brother and my husband bonded immediately due to a failure in the refrigeration system upon which depended Lawrance's delivery of twenty fresh-drawn turkeys to the Stork Club; Russ had had no good luck with turkeys either! Lawrance displayed a cavalier courage as the profit of a year's work vanished quite unpleasantly. Although supposedly on vacation, Russell stood by him until the disaster had been appropriately interred. More importantly, Lawrance and Russell sensed in each other a strong iconoclasm. It was a policy with Lawrance to defy icons. Russ just didn't see icons. Both became uncomfortable where something was presented as sacrosanct. Lawrance was known to faint at funerals!

On the few times Russ went to church with us, he always was a disgrace. I think, the last time, he put his head down on the back of the pew in front of him and took a nap during the sermon. He said he was just getting comfortable so he could listen better. I hasten to explain that Russ had not simply started up his truck and driven us to church. No. He had put on his suit, taken off his hat, and proceeded down to the quaint little Methodist Church for only one reason: to hear Holly sing, and because his coming in this case was predictable, though not a foregone conclusion, I had gone to some trouble to help Holly choose an acceptable hymn. Anyone who harkens to the words in the hymnal will observe the problem - especially at Easter. There tends to be a large complement of Christian soldiering and the blood of the lamb. For Holly and Russ, I found one of religion's sweetest love songs. *I went to the garden alone, when the dew was still on the roses...And He walked with me and he talked with me...*Holly's voice was so high and clear and effortless!

Lawrance became a novelist. He was always supportive of my trying to write, but didn't think I was much of a storyteller. "Nothing happens", he commented. I actually liked his writing - it seemed like mine - but his subject matter was so strange that no one in the family could give him the validation he longed for, especially not his mother. He got published, which I now understand is quite a remarkable feat, but he never had the artistic or economic success he felt he deserved. Many years later at a memorial gathering, his nine children, his two sisters, numerous nieces and nephews, and several of his wives spoke together for many hours about this controversial character in all of our lives.

Of that meeting, his son John - a lawyer now in Florida - writes:

> The get-together was hard for me but a necessary part of my grief. He's dead, and I fear nobody could be more astonished about that than he. He was a stranger to us, took very little interest in us, none at all in our children, and he made himself unpleasant to be with, deliberately, as if he wanted to be rejected. He got a lot out of the victim's position. It has been difficult, as Nick once said, to

love him and protect yourself at the same time. But I did love him and I know he loved us and would have shown us his love if he were not so afraid of...something, I am not sure what. So, wherever he may be, his fear is over and we carry on.

It is John who has become the "keeper of the archives" in my brother's family. "In his attic, where I went to find the Christmas tree stuff, I found instead a box full of Lawrance's novels and snippets of novels...a simple twist of fate. I decided I was strong enough to go through these books and see if I could relate to his effort. For the most part, it is incomprehensible, but when I read to find the man, rather than to be the judge, I find value there."

Three thousand miles has made a lively friendship difficult, but each time I meet my nieces and nephews I remember how much I like them.

CHAPTER TEN

What Children Do

Back at the ranch. When my children, isolated at home in the countryside, needed the company of other children, Jeanne Sullivan (a rancher with a teacher's credential) and I started a play school in an old war surplus quonset hut located in a field near the town of Potter Valley. When our children needed a creative outlet, I joined the PTA and helped to organize talent shows and Halloween costume parades safely in the Grange Hall. When our children needed protection from the violence they were seeing in school, Russell joined the school board and helped to eliminate corporal punishment. No swatting kids with the blackboard pointers. When we wanted to dance, we took our music player, a heavy box Wollensack reel-to-reel tape recorder, and our loudspeakers to the Grange Hall and Russell directed the band - Guy Lombardo's!

Gradually Russell's back faltered, chancy from a childhood bout with polio, the only case in 1911 in North Dakota. He reached adulthood with one crippled leg - a surgically remade foot on the end of two bones with little muscle. This is not easy to describe because his walk appeared more jaunty than limping, and he was the best "ballroom dancer" on the Grange Hall's polished, inlaid wood floor. Eventually it became too hard for him to hike the hills; rather than turn his ankle, he had to do most of his cattle handling on horseback, and counted on the help of the black-and-white McNab shepherds he trained himself, as best he could - or more rightly, as best they would. They were cow dogs or they were not - not deer dogs, not rabbit dogs. Russ found himself screaming at them when, rowdy as schoolboys, they drove his cattle through his fences. "Come up! Toughie! Peggy! Jack! Damn it! Come up! I'll break every bone in your body!" It was a quotation;

89

he never laid a hand on a one of them. You have no cow dogs at all - no way - if they don't love to herd cows!

It was a life, challenging as marriage, but we could not parlay the love for eighteen hundred acres of Mendocino upland into simple subsistence. Russ became pragmatic - maybe only at long last. He had learned the rancher's trade, relished it, plied it well and unstintingly, and in spite of a wife whose name appeared on Henry Wallace's Independent Progressive Party ballot, earned the respect of his neighbors in the corral and on the school board. But he would not get in the saddle at dawn, endure the filaree stickers reaching through the eyelets of his boots, lie in the mud to hold a calf for vaccinating and branding...all just for scenery and romance. After sixteen years, we put the ranch up for sale.

For a whole year - after our weathering such a hard decision - there were no buyers, not even lookers. All the tasks and chores felt different without the special energy in our earlier hopes, but I was determined that we would keep the life intact; I was determined that we would not be the ones to subdivide a way of work some other family might thrive on. Then one buyer appeared. His name was Vermillion. He came from well-to-do suburban Atherton, seeking the rural life for his family that teetered on the brink with drugs and alcohol. He, and we, thought he had found what was needed, but Potter Valley - in its simplicity, a throwback even when we found it years before - had changed. It did not offer escape. The first year of Vermillion's ownership, the house burned down. No longer could I revisit the backdrop, once unchanging behind the transformations of our four children growing. From now on, I would be at the mercy of a few indoor photos and memories rashly crayoned in my mind, as in a child's coloring book, paying no attention to staying within the black, solid lines. And Frank Vermillion learned that the little country schools were no longer immune to the world's dis-ease. Alcohol and drugs found children in Potter Valley, too. The ranch sold, and sold again, and again, its price skyrocketing as it became twenty-acre plots on which to live happily ever after, "on the land"! It seems now, needlessly, I always interfered with Russ's chance to make money without strenuous physical work.

We decided to move to Ukiah. We were familiar with Ukiah. It was the town that had music teachers, movie theaters, roller skating rinks, and a high school with a more diverse faculty than the small community high school in Potter Valley. Even though I had chosen *downward mobility* for myself, I still valued a richer cultural opportunity for my children. My two oldest daughters commuted for an hour to Ukiah High School in the years prior to us moving out of Potter Valley. This created some bad feelings between us and the Potter Valley high school educators, but I was acutely aware that our girls longed for an active drama and music department. And if these longings were not fulfilled, they would direct them to teenage boys. More than one child in the valley gave birth at fifteen.

Perhaps these "longings" were also mine, growing out of the years of witnessing - at first, with surprise - the dramatic play in our ranch kitchen, and later, in the local talent shows. (I urged that we would never call them talent contests! The performing arts are not a competitive sport!) I recall one time - it was Halloween and the celebration was made much of to discourage hazardous "tricks." There would be "treats" prepared by the ladies of the Grange. There would be door prizes and prizes for the best disguise. Everybody went. The costumed children were pushing and shoving each other excitedly as they paraded across the stage. Russell and I craned our necks to find Timi, then only four years old. In her moment front-and-center, she stepped forward from her companions and "performed" a gesture: ta-dah! It was a first clue that she would reach beyond our hearth to a career in acting and directing. But the breadth of her work could not be prefigured by a child's performing flair. Timothy would infuse her creative goals with a country aesthetic and her parents' good old union values. In her production of *The Rainmaker* at The Guthrie Theater in Minneapolis, she cast Starbuck as a Native American, inviting audiences to wonder whether he might really be a rainmaker, displaced from his land and culture. And her Lizzie was directed to show a feminist aesthetic - not a spinster, but a woman who had yet to find a man worth marrying. Timothy worked as an actress for many years but given the limited number of powerful roles created for women, she discovered she had more influence and freedom to present a vision as a director than she did as an actor. Timothy is now the Artistic Director at the San Jose Repertory Theatre, where she has made a commitment to present plays that challenge the audience to imagine a better world. However, occasionally Timothy still performs and I see the sparkle that caught my attention in the Halloween parade so many years ago.

I have to confess to myself that when I see my children on stage, it is the fulfillment of a mother's dream, assiduously repressed by a sense of decency. I did not want to be a "stage mother" such as a few I had met while teaching at The Professional Children's School on Broadway in New York. Rather, I wanted to emulate the ones I met who were devoted parents struggling with the conflicts and contradictions of their helping role. The truth is, I did not escape this role, and it was often fraught with anguish I had not anticipated. I could not find a comfortable place between laissez-faire as childhood's birthright, and providing the support - or even discipline - a youngster needs while embarking on the path to excellence, whether in playing basketball or the piano or in the performing arts.

I will never forget a trip to the Northern California town of Laytonville where Holly was to receive a Bank of America Award for Achievement in the Fine Arts - an honor that required an acceptance speech in competition with other candidates from Northern California high schools. Holly was right in the middle of the three-performance run of *My Fair Lady*. We drove in total silence, "vocal rest," which did not seem restful to two people who tend to be talkative together - while I raged secretly at a high school music director who would dangle such seductive opportunities in front of students with multiple responsibilities in their senior year, not yet old enough to look out for themselves. I fumed unfairly. I went to the library and asked them to order me books that addressed care of the voice. They came up with text by singers from Eartha Kitt to Gallicurci, and in a book by Joseph Hofmann an invaluable line, "Who says I play the piano with my fingers"...or sing with my throat?"

Actually, there was a lot I didn't understand, biased by motherly concern. The high school was faced with the challenge of what to do for - or with - many students whose needs it was failing to meet and didn't know how to meet. They called them hoods. "Put them in the music department!" Many youngsters at the rehearsals were economically deprived or had homes so fraught with argument that they were glad to have another place to be in the evenings. To his credit, the impresario, Les Johnson, overlooked a lot of unmusical behavior and kept his eye on the goal of producing "musicals" - thus introducing many children to the words and tunes of a uniquely American art form. Still, in hindsight, I know now that *Annie Get Your Gun* did not qualify as a cross-cultural expression, in a school community with many Native American students.

I watched my child sing her heart out, belting the melodies and rhythms so that kids in the chorus could get a handle on it - on this, their command performance. And I saw Holly inspired by a companionship she had not known; it was a creative exchange. By curtain time, she was acting her way through My Fair Lady in order to persuade a spent voice to last out the three performances. I did not get to hear "*I Could Have Danced All Night*" and "*Wouldn't It Be Loverly*" in the open-throat tones enjoyed by a handful of tired parents waiting through long-lasting, after-school rehearsals in a cold auditorium. However, I was perhaps the only one disappointed. Someone told me, "Forever after, Eliza will look like Holly Near."

Holly inherited her father's natural singing voice. (He joked that if someone had gotten a-hold of him earlier, he could have been Bing Crosby.) He could have been himself! Although Holly loved Broadway musicals and knew so many by heart, she abandoned a formal theatrical career for the life of a troubadour for peace and justice, passionately uniting with "the hoods of the world", the marchers, the demonstrators, the audiences with a cause.

However, Ukiah was a invaluable practice ground for my children and the presence of the very talented Jeff Langley, pianist/composer/student leader, opened up opportunities to young singers because of his extraordinary respect for the female voice. Both Laurel and Holly worked with Jeff in their high school years. And we the parents, the students, the community were the lucky audience that got to watch them practice in innumerable non-competitive shows.

There is a performance aspect to athletics, too - that is, when parents come in. My son, Fred, was a natural athlete - soloist and team player. To my surprise, Russell canceled all his sacrosanct appointments to attend the baseball game if Fred was playing. I struggled with my pride in conflict with my dislike of competition that required some little fellows to sit warming the bench throughout a "game." The coach says, "Winning isn't important, it's everything!" The parents say, "Come on, Teach! Everybody plays!" I trusted Fred to work this out for himself, knowing that he would cringe if I intervened. The moment arrived when a Ukiah coach pushed an overweight lad too far, humiliating the already exhausted boy, demanding that he do an extra lap because he had not run fast enough. Fred, who seemed slated to play first string in every sport forever after, decided to play no more. He found new friends, like Holly did, among "the hoods."

I often heard my husband make the pronouncement that to build a house is an elemental task every man worth his salt must perform. I would not have so insisted - no one in my family had done this - but perhaps a little boy heard and signed on. In any case, Fred is now a carpenter in San Francisco, but he has not entirely eluded the performing arts. He takes his son to Little League and to the ski slopes and gymnastics and piano lessons. What's more, his partner is Krissy Keefer, one of the founders of The Wallflower Order Dance Collective, and currently co-director of The Dance Brigade in Oakland, California. Fred works behind the scene handling the heaviest props, building the sets; literally, he has supported the performing arts since he gave up his own sturdy, vigorous participation at the age of six, after he had learned better in school. Fred and Krissy now have a daughter. Fred divides his time between parenting and working on the beautiful houses of the San Francisco bay area, some of which were destroyed in the fires and earthquakes that plague the Northern California hills. A week after the baby was born, Krissy was back on her feet directing the annual holiday special, *The Revolutionary Nutcracker Sweetie!* I look at my new granddaughter and wonder, will she be a carpenter or a dancer?...or pursue some trade that has yet to be heard of in 1992?

Our youngest daughter, Laurel, is also a dancer. Laurel and Krissy are best friends and co-founders of The Wallflower

Order Dance Collective. Laurel began studying dance at San Jose State and then moved to Eugene, Oregon, Wallflower's first home. What is that name! Wallflower Order! One word suggests a bonding among women who have been left on the sidelines - wallflowers. Order is variously evocative; perhaps order is the cause and the process and the end-product of all art. Whatever, it is their name.

Although I had gone to Bennington College where dance - innovatively, at the time - was an accrediting part of the curriculum, I was unprepared to keep up with these five young women as they rehearsed in freezing halls - one space went by the acronym, WOW Hall - endured bleeding feet as they ran barefoot across splintery stages, worked part-time as waitresses, drove cross-country in an old Rambler American, slept on the floors, and lived off of coffee and tofu. They danced of American peasants, of desperate immigrants in modern America, and of mothers giving birth. The members were highly differentiated, with all in a well-conceived choreographic unit. To me Laurel contributed a sense of theater, the loveliness of life, the mystery of birth and death, the magic of nature - breezes, treetops and wordless airy happiness in motion, contrasting with Krissy's ballet-trained, land-touch, graceful muscularity and magnificent humor. Lyn, Alex, Linda, Laurel, Krissy! I see you in motion.

Years later, when the collective dissolved, Krissy and one of the other dancers, Nina, formed a new dance company, taking on a more militant name that was inspired by solidarity work with Latin America, The Dance Brigade. Naming!

Annually, they produce a show called *Furious Feet*, which showcases the work of many dancers - a group from Chile, a "differently abled" group which performs in wheelchairs, an Asian troupe, a Native American troupe. A multicultural dance company themselves, Dance Brigade also performs its own wonderful choreography, tinged with acerbic political comment.

Six years of cruising in the vehicles of the alternative culture (which I understood to mean culture independent of commercial censorship and mainstream limitations, that is, poor!) was probably reason enough for Laurel to seek a change in her professional focus, but I believed there were other compelling considerations beside money. There was the desire to build family

95

and community which can be celebrated but not personally realized when one is a traveler.

Time and historical context reinforced change of direction for many young people. The mind-blowing self-discovery in women's culture had spread like wildfire, even as it was berated, ignored, and/or denied by the male-dominated critics and historians. Both men and women on the outer edges participated in creating an artistic response to what women had revealed. The crisis of innovation subsided. Now came the complex work of maintaining a feminist/humanist perspective...moving what had once been radical into mainstream culture. At a meeting of women writers in 1992 a woman said, "Men preempted our insights - as ever."

Coincidentally, from coast to coast, innovators in spirit were yearning for a closer touch with earth and weather to be savored by growing their own food. They bought land they could afford, sometimes more barren than they recognized in the green delusions of California's spring-in-November. They built uniquely handcrafted cabins and found ways to farm land we would have deemed not arable. The technology making it possible to dig deep wells, and the philosophical commitment to an environment uncluttered by the artifacts of an extravagant civilization, combined to foster their "dubious journey", on the land.

Laurel had long dreamed of living out in the hills. Someday her sons will be inspired by remembering that they entered earth in such a wild mountainscape, home of raccoons and white deer and a natural birth. Some years later Laurel found her way back to town and began to find a home for her dance and her love of children in the community of Ukiah. It is hard to find a job in Mendocino County; you have to make the best ones up. Her dance company is called Earth Trek. She writes, choreographs, produces and performs plays for children like her works, *With Two Wings*, and *Courage Parade*, earning the gratitude of many parents endlessly in search of meaningful, creative outlets for their children.

Then came *Sleepwalker*, a piece she wrote and performed with Krissy Keefer, rich in dance, comedy and tender remorse, considering that it explores the contemporary aches of alcoholism, co-dependency, and relationship addiction.

For readers like myself, not familiar with this terminology, relationship addiction means rushing compulsively from one love to another. The burden is on the rusher, and not on the faults of the rushed from. Laurel's alcoholic woman created an inexpressible sadness arcing between her and every soul beyond the stage. Sleepwalker was sponsored by the Zellerbach Family Fund and has a future with both school and community audiences...the subject is miserably timeless. Laurel has founded a school of dance, employing four more teachers of different techniques, giving the children experience with a wide variety of styles.

Laurel developed a summer performing arts program for young people with Paulette Arnold; it has a long waiting list. Laurel also choreographs for the high school and the Ukiah Playhouse. She has founded a dance school, employing four teachers with richly differing backgrounds. I watch young people "discover" her, the way we young Bennington women "discovered" our cultural heros and heroines.

These are my children but as Kahlil Gibran's poem says, put beautifully to music by Esaye Barnwell and sung by Sweet Honey in The Rock, "Your children are not your children, they are the sons and the daughters of life longing for itself."

My mother achieved great likeness in portraiture, as seen in these drawings of Fred, Sr. and Timothy, and watercolors of my children.

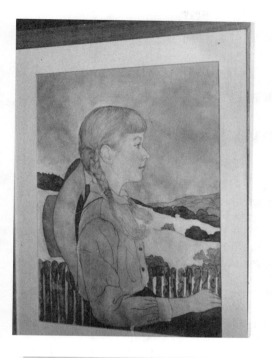

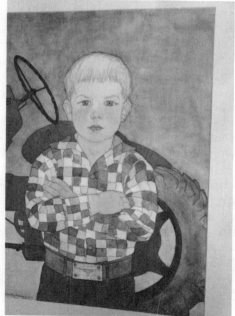

CHAPTER ELEVEN

Doolan Canyon, Ukiah

I see where my children have gone, and now I know it was right for us to leave Potter Valley. Russell was surely not tired of ranching, but he sensed that our children needed a stepping stone from which to leap to their next choices. With a pocketful of cash, which was perhaps no more than we had come with years before - the vertiginous rise in land values was still around the corner - Russell chose a sweet place in Ukiah called Doolan Canyon just on the edge of town; a swimming pool allowed six giant redwood trees to scatter their seeds in the aqua-blue water, causing an addition to my housekeeping far more time-consuming than had been my sweeping out of mud from ranchers' boots. It was not my idea of moving to town, but it was Russell's turn to choose. I had looked forward to a noisy, busy, working-class street where I could achieve the identity that had lured me from Park Avenue in New York City. Mine was not Russell's geography. His childhood had been played out as a banker's son, but in a very small town in North Dakota. He imagined himself now as a gracious host to the young people who would be our children's friends in circumstances less isolated than Beach, North Dakota, or Potter Valley, California - but this was not to be. Alcohol and drugs were warping the possibility of generous hospitality. A carload of youngsters had left the party of a well-liked family and had died ten minutes later speeding on a straightaway within a few miles of home. How come? No intoxicants had been served - but no one had thrown a spotlight on the parking lot or opened car trunks or counted what was missing from parents' liquor cabinets nor weighed the intoxicating qualities of sexual excitement that accompany the blending of adolescence and automobiles. Our children did not want to lay this sorry risk on their parents; others must have felt the same way, for parties moved to the anonymity of vineyards, orchards, and riverbanks. My son told me with gentle candor for a man of fifteen, "Remember, Mom, I'll be doin' my best - but I must be with my friends. I will be with my friends!" He lived. We left Doolan Canyon after a dozen years. I think of those days as of a party that never quite came off.

Still, there is a lot to remember about the time when we lived in Doolan Canyon from 1963 to 1979 - a true canyon, cool in summer, cold in winter when the sun didn't even try to get over the hills.

It was here that television entered our lives; thirty years later, I am still evaluating the significance of the flood of experience that, at the touch of a button, overwhelms whatever else is going on in the room. My little grandsons give it attention a teacher would envy and sometimes even weep when it is withheld by their mother in favor of live life. But back then, it was a family social event when we gathered to watch "The Dean Martin Show," "The Ed Sullivan Show," "The Lawrence Welk Show," or "The Andy Williams Show." It was also a medium to be honored for its ability to bring global news into homes around the world...even though those corporations who controlled the advertisements had great power over what stories were told and how they were told. We read in the papers about Civil Rights, but were it not for television, we would not have known what a civil rights march looked like...except for the few we drove a hundred miles to take part in.

It was in Doolan Canyon that I began to enter a new community through painstakingly written letters to the editor. I defined myself in print...taking sides on current issues, local and global. I responded to the war being waged in Vietnam, commented on world hunger as well as poverty in our own hometown, hesitantly quoted feminist ideas as I began to be affected by the women's movement, expressed my sorrow over environmental chaos, supported the creativity of our local artists, disapproved of aid sent to Latin American dictators, and voiced my rage at the death penalty. My children tell me they began to know the morning sounds as a mixture of the canyon birds in the redwoods and the typewriter down the hall.

It was from Doolan Canyon that Timothy came and went - to San Francisco State, to modeling school, to theater studies at The London Academy of Music and Drama (LAMDA), and to a theater she joined in San Francisco, the Circus Theater. Russell and I, and sometimes the other children, would drive down to see what our eldest daughter was up to. It was often startling and challenging, and it was always a surprise to me that this tall, dark, powerful, bold, funny woman had come from me. People question me about my children. "They take after their father," I explain.

It was when we lived at Doolan Canyon that I discovered an experimental college in Nevada that might challenge my son, Fred, who, like so many of his peers, had found nothing to be excited about in school. The college shut down before it had its chance at his mind. It was also from Doolan Canyon, beneath the majesty of our Redwood trees, that the implications of the draft entered our lives. Was there a right to refuse to kill? Was <u>refusal</u> not an individual liberty of a sacred order? A guest speaker at our church told her story: she was a member of a long-time pacifist family. She had gone around publicly speaking against the draft, and helping young people decide whether they should go to prison - with all the dangers that threatened young men - or flee to Canada, renouncing, perhaps forever, their right to stand proudly in their homeland. Her own son, at the last minute, foreswore his mother's words, proclaiming that she had used him to promote her own views. He enlisted.

Fred arrived at draft age. I was most reluctant to usurp my son's moment of decision. I believed that each life has but a few moments - or maybe none - when it is representational of major truth, where a clear choice exemplifies the nature of the soul. While I grieved that such life and death options should be presented to a lighthearted teenager who still knew how to play, I kept silent. Not so, his sisters! "Over my dead body, will he be sent to die or kill in Vietnam!" Fred never had to make an overt choice: his draft number arrived and it was very high, never to be reached unless the war went on and on and on. I do not know whether secretly or with his friends he rehearsed the agony of an imminent decision, or simply expected to take on whatever came down the pike. At the time, I thought the latter was more his way.

102

But over the years, I have witnessed in him a quiet, intelligent, undramatic opinion-forming, very much like his father's, short on fanfare.

It was from Doolan Canyon that I drove to board a little boat defying - sort of - the weapons-carrying ships moving out of Port Chicago in the Bay; that I walked for Peace and Economic Justice In Central America, for Equal Rights For Women, Self Determination, Gay Pride. What a community of walkers espousing each other's causes! I participated in founding Plowshares, dedicated to providing a free meal in Ukiah for anyone who could get to its dining room. No one must go to bed hungry...for all our sakes!

It was from Doolan Canyon that Russell and I entered a new phase of our life together. We joined forces once more and became "a record company"! Holly, living in Los Angeles, decided to record the antiwar songs she was writing and performing to passionate audiences; she was determined to do more than simply be "the entertainment" at rallies protesting the war in Southeast Asia. The major record companies noticed her popularity, but were not interested in her outspoken themes, so she and her writing partner, Jeff Langley, who also grew up in Mendocino County, decided to make a record independently. Holly and Jeff were old friends; Jeff had played Pickering to Holly's Eliza in *My Fair Lady*. Jeff and Holly made a record called *Hang In There*; they sold it to audiences after each concert, but they needed someone to oversee the mail-order distribution. They needed someone with an address. Holly assured us that there would only be a dozen or so orders a month to send out. We agreed, Doolan Canyon would be fine. And we were delighted to help. This would be our antiwar work; Holly called her nascent company Redwood Records.

Russell devised a set of books, and I set up a packing and shipping system. This was a primitive operation; I sprained my thumb repeatedly cutting the corrugated cardboard covers with a large pair of scissors, and we carried the albums by the armload to the local United Parcel Service. But Holly had miscalculated; after the orders for *Hang In There* passed the two thousand mark, Russell and I created slightly more sophisticated systems. Records were mailed directly from the manufacturer. I learned to talk to record stores and distributors from San Francisco to Berlin. I answered mail and we discovered a new language doing "quality control." This time we weren't making airplanes for the war effort. We were shipping music for the peace effort.

As Redwood Records grew, it was no longer a single-artist endeavor. Redwood, in Holly's mode, became a company dedicated to distributing the music of other artists who sang for peace...and feminism. As the women's movement grew - unfurled might be a better word - Holly, and we too, felt that she needed to bring in a group of women who had been working in the middle of the feminist and lesbian movements to help implement the vision of Redwood. This was a testing time for Holly as she made her way through new and revolutionary ideas. She was not one to skip over the hard parts as she actively sought answers to questions being raised across the country throughout the '70s like, "How can a feminist and an anti-imperialist artist in the USA cultural milieu be sensitive to global differences?" or "When is it appropriate for the confrontation of one oppression, like racism, to supersede the confrontation of another oppression, like sexism?" "How do issues of class divide women?" "How can artists invite people to acknowledge diversity in unity?" Holly felt the need to be surrounded by her peers in the search for answers. We moved out of the way to let this happen. Perhaps it was I more than Russell who supported this move. He was proud of his contribution to the distribution of radical culture and proud, too, of his bookkeeping, which he was loath to turn over to what at first was a less meticulous accounting. I felt it was ideologically embarrassing to have a woman-identified company rely on a man-parent to keep the tally. Holly never wanted to move Russell out of the way. It broke her heart to have to choose, but history pushes hard sometimes. And Russell, remembering his own union days, understood this better than most.

Russell and I invited Redwood Records to take permanent residence in Doolan Canyon, and we moved downtown. After a few years, Redwood's growth pushed it again, this time toward the city where ideas tend to prosper in good company. Twenty years later, it is now a flourishing non-profit arts organization in Oakland, California, unique in its local, national, and international commitment to supporting diversity through music.

104

CHAPTER TWELVE

"Downwardly Mobile"

Since this is a story about *downward mobility* - the concept is both expanding and contracting unmercifully - I must not forget to notice where my reputed fortune went. The question was never integral to my decisions: I did what I wanted to, and had all I wanted, and never came anywhere near the end of my rope, being of modest aspiration. So, where? The simplest theorem is that if you don't use money to make money, it evaporates. Q.E.D. There were other factors. We grew up confident that we would always be rich; it was a reassuring psychological slant that I do not deplore, regardless of the outcome. However, my mother became trapped for many years in a situation that, to her dismay and sense of helplessness, actually used up a lot of the money she had looked forward to leaving to her children, children to whom she was always giving so much that the image of benefactor was a habit with her. Apparently this is an inherited characteristic, like brown eyes; in working-class families, it is the children who expect to provide for the parents. In my determination to be *downwardly mobile*, I neglected to factor in the pain of not being able to help my children much.

My mother chose a darling little house on a cobbled street a few blocks from Rittenhouse Square in Philadelphia. It was a short stroll for Ruth, who was raising six children in a five-tier home on downtown Locust Street, and a son-in-law who was a brilliant and controversial city planner, Ed Bacon, spokesman for neighborhoods rather than "housing developments." The whole scene was a perfect base from which my mother could sally forth to Sanibel Island, to Mazatlan, Guatemala, or to a ranch in California.

Her children thought it was a perfect place for her to settle down and honor the talent she had been given by <u>working at it</u>, the talent of getting a likeness in portraiture. You never did that, Dorothy Smith Holmes! Today I seem to express my disapproval of her negligence by actually hanging eight of the portraits she did of my children, while a beloved Raoul Dufy print is stored in the shed. My mother's drawings have a pure and graceful line; there are no corrections, which is astonishing, considering the likeness she achieved; she "colored them" with a watercolor wash. (I do have on my walls an original work by local artist, Virginia Lien Fitch, and a furious portrait by Isaias Mata, of a Salvadoran woman holding her baby; there is a gun slung over her shoulder.)

Suddenly, my mother was imprisoned in her bed. She believed that she required nursing round the clock and the complementary services of a housemaid, a cook, a laundry woman, a bookkeeper, and a financial advisor, who surely did not attend to her affairs for free, although he was an old friend; in that world, most business is conducted with friends. All her children were glad that she had this help, as she had been brought up to expect. She would have been totally welcome to live with any one of us - but in our way. None of us wanted to have "servants." We thought our mother might even be better off "roughing it" with us; she would not be spending her last days with hired help as her closest allies. But they were good friends, the black women who worked for her, doing their jobs without supervision. With any one of her children, my mother would not have been so well taken care of. She could not have been the center of her world. She would not have been near her doctors. She would not have been able to ring for things. I asked myself, what on earth do poor people do when someone is old and ill in the family? They take care of each other within a bond mixed of duty, resentment, anguish, hopefully undamaged love, maybe neglect, surely guilt, probably chaos. I continued to adore the talks I had with my mother. Since she was quite deaf, it was hard to have our old confiding, with her "help" in the next room, unable not to listen, not to hear, and hard, too, to have my mother ring for one of these ladies to bring me a cup of coffee. Haven't I made airplanes!

What happened to my fortune? Whatever was left I spent along the way, I guess. While it was Russell's instinct to store away - my money, that is, for me - I believed in investing in skill development, in supporting every initiative the children had the energy and imagination and daring to take on; they could make their own livings...later. I am told, they received little warning from their parents about having to support themselves. The message they received was that the world was in fateful crisis and that they had a part to play if they could find the script.

This is not a story about my children - though mothers the world over will empathize with my preoccupation: I believe that each inherited a tendency to think more about making a life than a nest egg. When they make money - and they do - they never seem to use it to make more at "the bank." Rather, it becomes a resource - like their skills - to be spent in a chosen field. They all lead creative lives, working long hours, a few dollars away from impoverishment - while I dream of writing the all-American novel, publishing it in paperback, selling the rights to Hollywood where a hit movie will have parts for everyone and cause us all to live happily ever after!

Motherhood being what it is, I am happy with what the four people I must no longer call my children chose to do with the aptitudes they drew from the genetic pool, a spacious romping ground to grow up in without television, a large linoleum floor which looked as if it was made of wide, green boards to slide on and dance on barefoot without splinters, and above all a fine music system, seductive because they were allowed to handle the precious mechanisms of needle, turntable, and volume controls with their own little hands, long before recording tape cassettes became household tools. Perhaps there was a certain osmosis prevailing through the proximity of a mother schooled by the theater offerings of New York City in the '30s and a father who sang so sweetly at church, though also at home, when he had "hung a few on." All these elements are not inconsistent with *downward mobility* any more than is a career in the performing arts...although is it not here that we can also applaud rewards of astronomical proportions? Our nation's "royalty" are the stars of the silver screen, and I take pride in two in my family - Ruth and Ed's son, Kevin Bacon, and his wife, Kyra Sedgewick, both fine actors. I am always glad to see an artist well paid, and wish all were, and I must observe that no one of my children was particularly impressed by my ideological penchant for *downward mobility*, or as my daughter Timothy later described it, "mobile nobility." It was Necessity, the Mother of Invention, they harkened to the more.

When it comes to love, the daughters tended not to frequent sites where they could choose or be chosen by men likely to make a lot of money. They are more attracted to people who make things...if that word can include a play or a dance or a painting. Also, feminism changed what women "look for." One daughter found lesbianism to be an exciting and viable alternative to *he and she and baby makes three*. The women in my son's life have tended to be strong and independent with a world view and a working-class ethic.

Back to chronology! In Potter Valley, Russell and I began to realize that we had not given our children a hometown where they could stay and earn a living in occupations they had practiced for...the performing arts and cattle ranching. In Potter Valley, The Grange or Farm Bureau or Progress Club thought singing and dancing looked like so much fun, no youngster would be paid to be "the entertainment" - although boys were paid for pumping gas and loading hay. Further, one of our kids developed an allergy. We began to notice a rhythmical wheezing in the house, largely covered up by a merrier cacophony. Which kid? The boy! Which allergy? The pollen of wheat, oats, grasses, and animal danders - an allergy to country work. We had raised all of our children to leave home!

As everywhere in California, there has since been much development, but it is still not easy to find a job in Mendocino County, what with the redwood timber industry faltering from its own excesses in grabbing the pristine forest, and faced by an increasingly vocal ecological consciousness warning that clear-cut timbering is not good for the land. A little lumber could build all the houses we need; trees growing here are not to be exploited for export-profit. Useful pay/work must be found for displaced loggers. They cry, "My job! My job!" - as if there were a God-given right to go on doing the wrong thing. Like a rancher's overgrazing, overlogging cannot be allowed, lest the hardly arable hills wash down to the river and out to the sea, leaving behind bare crags. The tragedy of conflicting interests affecting rock-bottom family livelihood became exacerbated by the unsolved mystery of a bomb exploded in the car of popular environmentalists who were promoting Redwood Summer on behalf of saving old-growth redwood trees. The journey into terror for these two young people, Judi Bari and Darryl Cherney, may prove useful; timber owners are now making public their plans for managing a renewable resource, acknowledging the accountability factor in the private ownership of a national treasure. This would indeed be upwardly mobile, whether or not there proves to be such a thing as "sustainable yield," fall a tree, plant a tree! Well, maybe. But conflict abounds in Mendocino County; it is not, as once believed, an escape route to paradise. Masonite, the largest employer, has smokestacks that clearly emit more than steam for all to see. Environmentalists cry, "pollution!" and the company, feeling threatened, speaks of moving away to a country where there is less control, less demand for costly emission reduction technology. It is nothing new that workers' jobs are held hostage and whatever poor country receives the new industry will find their own children and environment threatened.

On a federal level, the nation's economy is propped up by a war economy. When it is suggested that we stop building weapons, the first line of concern raises the question, "But what about our jobs?" With all the humanitarian needs before us, there is no shortage of work that needs to be done. The question is whether corporations run by profit-obsessed chief executive officers can be persuaded to reorganize their priorities and production catalogues. *Out Now*, a California publication, estimates that, "The two and a half trillion we could save between now and the year 2,000 a.d. could bring life closer to resembling God's plan for a lot of folks."

Is it symptomatic of my *downward mobility* that I find myself speculating less about what people do than who they are? Many years ago, my daughter Timothy, when visiting family on the East Coast, wrote back in teenage perplexity, a ranch child, "They ask me what I do. Do I do anything?" Nonetheless, I know that any questions are gracious or at least attentive. I have lived where no one, no one at all, asked me what I found to do where I had come from. If I am asked today, sometimes I say I write - apparently an awesome or negligible occupation that closes off all smalltalk. Conversation goes better when I begin calling out the names, ages, and weights of grandchildren.

I do have grandchildren, and most are familiar with the details endlessly to be arranged in single-mother-head-of-household and single-father-head-of-household. Do these kids get to do the dishes in both kitchens or do they all eat out? More seriously, I notice many children today go home to two places made ready for them, with toys and clothes and neighbors, bus schedules, and TV Guides, and loving arms. Children are taking part in significant innovation. Parents who have decided to separate, who have come to the sad conclusion that "till death do us part" was a hope that did not prevail, now find themselves on the phone, on a daily basis, working out the children's packed agendas - these once dear parents who had reached a point where they could hardly talk to each other! More, in the work stress of double-households, parents cannot always be each other's child-care person. Quality child care beyond home has become, largely in absentia, a national issue, unaffordable on one salary - though undervalued and underpaid. Poetically, we aver that children are our national treasure, but our storage of this treasure is dismally casual.

In the undoing of the nuclear family - perhaps rightly so with all its inequitable roles - we have not yet come to a time when we've replaced that structure with something new, designed to help parents, and in particular women, and most essentially children on the journey of growing up. No one, but certainly not parents and children, does well in isolation. People thrive on cooperation. Our nation is in grave danger until we creatively face the question of the new family. People should not have to choose between their desire to do creative work and their desire to parent. In the early days, there were unaffianced women with not good options outside the home; there was no job opening for them as doctor or astronaut. They were counted on for child care, as were immigrant women getting started in America - like Kate. There will always be women - and men - who love to care for children if they are not insulted by the low value and low pay

110

society assigns to an enormously imaginative task: preparing children to be all they can be in 2001.

Timothy waits for an anti-nuclear demonstration to begin - having often performed at rallies, my children bring art to politics and politics to art.

PHOTO BY LARRY MELIOUS

Krissy Keefer, my daughter-in-law...
always a touch of Erin in our family
life.

PHOTO BY FRED NEAR

Laurel and Krissy in their production of
Sleepwalker.

Laurel

Fred

PHOTO BY JANET ORR

Timothy, Artistic Director of the San Jose
Repertory Theatre.

Ruth's husband, Ed Bacon.

PHOTO BY IRENE YOUNG

Holly sings at a rally for Choice.

CHAPTER THIRTEEN

Raising Sheep in Hopland

I am getting ahead of my story. After leaving our ranch in Potter Valley in 1963, Russell turned to selling ranch properties. For sure, he knew hill and vale; he said it was all he knew. I disagreed. How could he say that, he who had worked a ranch nigh on to twenty years; he could have qualified as a mechanic or a midwife! I turned away, suddenly deprived of a woman's traditional motivation in her husband's occupation. He had become a real estate broker surrounded by salespeople. My father had been a real estate broker selling estates in New York; I had not come to California to help sell it but rather, in wartime, to save it...from invasion, and now, postwar, to save it from random, planless subdivision bereft of the organic development of a bona fide town, growing from its own history. Feeling deprived, I began to write.

Years earlier, I had put that proclivity away, shocked when I found myself resenting my "little darlings" interruptions. Now, I began by jotting down every detail about the work Russ had performed as a cowman, and every growing thing I could identify in Mendocino County, California. A long book emerged. It has since been pared down and pared down again, but it has not found a publisher; maybe it never will. I am only now seeing what it is about - if one can accurately ascribe themes to a story. It is called *Time Out*. Its cast of characters is beset with questions about race and who owns the land and whether a moral man must stay in the fray for social justice or maybe take time out to live the life revolutions are fought for, if he gets the chance. Surely there are more current metaphors for these areas of conscience - but still, I love my words.

Russell and I moved downtown into a little house he had come by in a real estate transaction. I had been afraid of this house, afraid we would end up living in it. Apparently there was an aesthetic component in my commitment to *downward mobility*. Maybe this was why it did not work out. There were other reasons. Although Russell had demonstrated his old energy and versatility in now becoming a broker, teaching himself the rigorous rules just being developed around property exchange, he wearied of the endless specifications that interfered with the genuine joy he took in helping people at that special moment when they would find a home. He began to stay away from the office, only supervising the contracts of his agents and spending a lot of time with home-hunters who were mostly tourists. He was a tour-guide to people changing their lives. He helped them believe that this was worthwhile and could be done. He was almost a psychotherapist to the new pioneers.

While I was shyly enjoying the welcome in women's groups such as the League of Women Voters, there seemed to be no similar way of associating for him, for men, unless one was an Elk or a Lion. Men's way - if they were not joiners - was to share a drink; the bar was a casual clubhouse, open without formal invitation, the only place to be trusted for ever-ready camaraderie. Russ loved the bar scene. He also became drinking buddies with a Mexican family - apparently many families inhabiting one small house across the street from ours. Russell did not know their language, which was just as good because he suspected their housing had legal problems, so many young men came at evening to sleep and were gone at sun-up. The bond was in the bottle. Russ felt good in their home with the little children allowed to climb up on his lap, and the young immigrant men saw the presence of a nice American guy in their house as a good omen. I became worried when the party moved to our house, and the tots were wandering back and forth across the street unsupervised with cars whizzing by while I was at a meeting and Russ shared a bottle. I came to believe we should go back to the country, to a setting in which our differing ways of life had once found compatibility. To this idea Russ was more amenable than freshly enthusiastic, and this caused me to acknowledge that the same could be said of all the major moves we had made together. Well, one more time!

After driving around the country side for a while, we happened on a little sheep ranch for sale - just twenty acres, where Potter

Valley we had cared for eighteen hundred - at the end of an old-fashioned, sweet and narrow, winding lane. Perfect! No sooner had we bought it and moved in than I comprehended the demography: it would be over this road that Russ would come home at night, after spending a few hours at the congenial country bar of Hopland. What had I set up!

I recount these pedestrian sequences in order to think about the fact that alcohol use is crucial in humble lives as ours, but also in the councils of the world's governance. I'm appalled to think that world leaders may make domestic and foreign policy while suffering from the dysfunction of addiction. Did Russell's alcoholic dreams fly higher than my sober ones? Well, we'll never have the chance to know. Smiling happily, he would ask, "Call this a problem?" And then he would instruct me to cut the ram from the flock in an open field or put on a shoulder-tank and start out for the mountain ridge where a wildfire was burning out of control; I lost my sense of humor. There is a substantial grassroots movement to abjure the use of "spirits." It is quite different from the "Prohibition" legislated in my youth, and neither is it like the voluntary quitting of smoking, largely impelled by fear in those who smoke and those who always knew it was deleterious to be with a smoker. The end of alcohol abuse - or maybe even use - will only come as each individual perceives that life is more beautiful or usable when not seen through this prism. There will have to be enormous and imaginative changes in the economic and social system for "life" to qualify.

At Hopland, as thirty years ago when we came to the ranch in Potter Valley, I watched Russell teach himself his way around new acres and new animals. Sheep are not like cows - and he remembered how North Dakota farmers hated sheep because they cropped the grasses down to the mud and then jerked them out by the roots. But today was California in 1979, and Russell found the sheep that came with the ranch to be amusingly personable - not at all alike as sheep. My son-in-law did a portrait in cut-glass of the old ewe; we could actually recognize her. It still hangs in my window! Indeed, the lambs did gambol as the poets promised, and only when they were afraid did the sheep move as a group, not aimlessly, miraculously in unison, veering this way or that in waves without visible communication. Russ learned to shear their wool and trim their hooves and doctor their runny noses. Instead of being repelled, he practiced liking them. It was a very good time for us, tinged with irreparable sadness when alcohol put many of the lovely incidents of rural living askew. Our children, delighted to find us back on a farm, came visiting, but it was hard for one daughter or another to accept a changed person in the place of the mostly sober, always handsome, laughing, vigorous father they had grown up with. Some two years later, my husband died of an aortic aneurysm. I had never heard those words and I do not know if there is a cause of death hidden in the pages of life and shielded from view by medical names. Why is it that when one loses a longtime partner, one feels self-reproach in a bottomless way?

I stayed on in Hopland. Alone one day, high on a hill and under a familiar oak, I scattered the ashes and bits of bone the mortuary had handed me in a brown paper bag. Then I traced the paths that Russ and I had stepped out together. Wifely, I had watched but not insisted on a chance to learn-by-chance to learn-by-doing, as they say in pedagogical circles. I had not plowed or disced or harrowed or mowed or raked the hay into windrows for the baler to pick up. I did not know if I could take his place on the tractor seat, but in fact, I tried. Wistfully, I filled its tank with gas and used the grease-gun on its crucial fittings. I put in a crop of oats and vetch. I herded the sheep from barn to pasture, watching over the new lambs that arrived in the spring. I fixed the fence. I wrapped the pipes in winter to keep them from freezing over and cut the wild grass in summer, to protect the farm from brushfires. I carried in wood to keep the stove burning and I wrote...not much.

One night when I was at a concert in San Francisco, somebody's pet dog got loose, surely with its friend, and killed or maimed most of my sheep. Returning before dawn, I felt the eerie presence of death, and the despair in the whimpering of my dogs that advisedly I had left tied, helpless in my lack of trust in them. The devastation was partly attributable to ignorance; city people had been allowed to buy small parcels of the neighboring five-thousand-acre ranch, recently purchased by a speculator who had no truly agricultural intentions. These new folks had looked forward to moving to the country where the family dog could romp. They had no notion what the family dog could do...and no one stopped to acknowledge what he had done. I felt profoundly hurt by this. Of necessity, the woolly carcasses lay where they had been strewn, where my neighbors had to see them as they drove by. It is not possible that the culprits were unknown, but no one told. For the first and only time, I was glad that Russell was not with me. My childhood remembrance of the advice, don't be a squealer stared down my sense of being wronged; I did not want to stand helplessly in the road as people stopped to say they were sorry, and then drove on without telling. Did they think a woman had no right to run a ranch? And I felt guilty, too, that I had not protected the animals in my care. Their being "mine" seemed part of a contract...broken.

My nephew Fred came from his job at HUD in San Francisco to give tetanus shots to the surviving sheep, and my son Fred used the tractor tools to dig a mass grave. I had seven sheep left. I lived morosely, minimally inspired when the sun came up, and listening for the moving sound of a dog on the loose; he would come back for the rest. After a few months, a woman arrived from Petaluma; she had goats and thought mine was the place of their dreams and hers. Perhaps it was. I told her the whole story. At least, I thought, she knows as much as I do; there must be pets in Petaluma, too. She had a partner who said he knew everything; I was free to go.

In Hopland, Russell and I raised sheep. Al was our sheepdog.

Russell pulls the sickle through the grasses.

CHAPTER FOURTEEN

Arrived on Clay Street

No longer haunted by the theme of *downward mobility* - it was rapidly becoming inauspicious - I loaded all I would take with me on a large trailer and drove north on Highway 101, followed by my worldly goods. They looked poor and insignificant where I unloaded them in a storage unit, except for the desk on which I now write. This treasure had belonged to my uncle, George C. Smith, Jr. Long before it came to his use, the desk had been put together by craftsmen in New England, with two tiers of drawers on each side, ample knee-space, and a leather-covered work surface, gently cracked in the random patterns of antiquity, and now mostly sheltered by my typewriter and fluttering notes. It is alleged that this desk was shipped to China where it was decorated with the oriental representations of humans, plants, and animals, exquisitely painted in russet, parchment yellow, and highlights of aquamarine, then brought back around the Horn to be sold where New Englanders were thirsting after the exotic, having first created their own pure and simple household furnishing that would be so prized in future generations. I touch my desk and ask of it vast questions.

Pursuing friendly rumors about vacancy, I found a house for it and me on a broad street in a town such as I had seen so many times from Pullman coach trains, and wondered, "Who lives there? How do they happen to live there?" I had felt at home in more than one metropolis and in the countryside, but a small town seemed off limits, no way, not cool. I learned better. Ukiah was as engaging and representational of worldliness as New York City - what I saw of it - or Potter Valley or Hopland or San Francisco. People lived there, contemporary souls, loving and disputatious.

In my new abode with extravagantly high ceilings for its size and importance, there was no foundation or insulation, the porch was sagging, the wallpaper was peeling, the carpet moldy green, everything needed paint - tomorrow, because buying the house required a down payment equal to the down payment the goatbreeder had been able to come up with for the Hopland ranch. The heater was broken and it was cold enough to wear three California sweaters. Laurel came to share the space and the heat bill. We knew where to find wood, of course - having maintained rural connections - but when the city's natural gas became available, we decided that wood-burning fires were a romantic extravagance that depleted the efficacy of aerating leaves and added to the pall of smoke collecting over the town - only a certain kind of rambunctious breeze would blow it out of the hollow formed by the hills. Why do I hesitate to take down the chimney? Is it picturesque? Is it insurance against the total collapse of the "infrastructure"? I <u>will</u> take it down.

Doubling up in housing seems symbolic of our time, and a foretelling. There is money galore for inventing "smart bombs" to drop on other people, but little to build simple shelter for our own. Laurel is not one to board with her mother and make the contemporary compromises between her own mothering, earning a living, and maintaining her relationships...all under my gaze. Her living with me is a bona fide expedient - good for me, good for her, and good for the house, so she considers us and her two little boys a good team. Would it feel different if I were living with her? Of course! The arrangement would become part of an important political issue of our time reflecting a new population profile. <u>We are older</u>. It is said that one can judge a society by how it provides for its old people. I admit, it would feel *downwardly mobile* to me to live in "a home," in the exclusive company of folks over seventy-five, but neither do I wish to catch up on my reading while occupying rooms sorely needed by a growing family. I remember my own mother boasting that she loved to live with young people. Of course! But I am determined to spend a lot of time with old people, <u>people my age</u>, as we say when we are five. I am told, "You look so young!" On the contrary, this is what seventy-six looks like, given a life-long modicum of food, a little medicine, and enough of the tranquility all Creation deserves a measure of. We people in our seventies had better get together and talk; it's time to issue a report, having reached the age that used to be an end-goal. Then, as octogenarians, we can check out other roads to travel, interplanetary or mystic. I'll be ready to continue my dubious journey.

Can I still claim a penchant for *downward mobility*? In the '90s, laughter has slipped out of the words. Unemployment with its attendant poverty and terrifying inference that any single soul might not be needed somewhere in the fabric of the social totality, shames our land where *alabaster cities gleam, above the fruited plain.* The news has been semi-good about the world menu. We now know that no one need go hungry...if we share, if we direct planes and trains and ships to move harvests from where they are gleaned to wherever they are needed - meager, perhaps, but more if our society does not waste its breath duplicating the artifacts of war for profit; if someone is not always playing with fire. At last, all the creatures on Adam-and-Eve's no longer ignorant paradise can live every bit as well as Mankind, The Stewards, can imagine and devise...or Womankind!

Ah! But there is other news...as if the Truth were a function of revealing its opposite. I have just received a copy of a stunning baccalaureate address, delivered by an acquaintance and notable scholar, Elizabeth Shallcross Pool, in which she deplores a conspiracy of silence about the fact that Man is destroying his earth home by his exponential rate of population growth. Dr. Pool observes that a religiously inspired obsession with the abortion issue, including, strangely, opposition to funding of research to improve contraception, has repressed public discussion of the Planet's need to curb its population. She provides persuasive statistics to show that no improvement in agriculture or in energy efficiency, no pollution control, no water rationing can keep up with a world population doubling every thirty-nine years...A USA is added every 30 months! Population in the United States swelled from 150 million in 1950 to more than 225 million today. It is noted that wars, murderous as they have been, have never served to reduce population, and have often proved to effect the opposite. Elizabeth Pool implies that this tragedy has not been arrived at entirely by innocent libido; the dissemination of conception-prevention techniques is restricted, both at home and for export. Twice we have elected presidents politically opposed to even the discussion of population control. Why is this? The courting of the fundamentalist vote? The historical need for men to control women's reproductive choices, and therefore the workforce and the economy? The enormous income from Social Security? I had never thought of this sinful connection! Dr. Pool suggests another cause, perhaps the primary one: the fantastic success of the medical profession in wiping out disease. She challenges doctors to adopt a slogan: Save a life. Prevent a life!

It would be much more gripping to read Elizabeth Pool's books than my quotes from them, but I believe they are temporarily out of print. In the emergency, I can here divulge that her prescription might read, "No births at all for a while, and then a gradual reduction in our numbers to a level respectfully, knowledgeably, lovingly chosen...in regard to how many humans our dear Earth can sustain." I agree with this longtime population specialist that to do this "would, unquestionably, be the most difficult task ever elected by our species." Russell and I, one couple, added four to the generation following ours, and when two more potential mouths to feed - two more reproducers - were lost by miscarriage, I took on like a heartbroken failure of a woman. Indeed, change in attitude toward the most common experience - birth - has happened at an exponential rate.

Every woman must have the right to bear a child. Can this right be projected meaningfully to areas where there is little or no access to contraception or to family planning? How do we begin to think about teenage women so alone in the world that they have children so they will have someone to love them? Or women in war zones who have children to replace their dead sons and daughters? And there are lands where the poverty is such that women have many children in hopes that a few will live! And there are women so gifted in their love of children that their needs must have their way. It is written that the women of Greece refused to make love with their husbands until the men promised to forego war. Today likewise, women could create a powerful consensus for creating a society worthy of the miracle of a child.

Without painting my "white" face with *mea culpas*, I have walked along a lane in Mendocino County in "conspiracy" with

Native and Anglo friends who were demonstrating in protest of the local government's approval of an asphalt batch plant. It was to be placed adjacent to the already marginal allotment of infertile acres stingily granted to the taxpaying sons and daughters of human beings who once roamed free with deer and elk, rabbits, squirrels, chipmunks, gophers, foxes, wolves, bear - under majestic madrones, manzanita with the red bark so satiny to touch and fast to burn, and oaks with edible acorns, from which they learned to leach the poison by diverting a stream of river water to flow over sand basins filled with the mashed pulp. Earth, then, was awash with purest air, but the land was not "unused." People and animals already lived there; it was not up for grabs!

It's Columbus Day.

In telling of my dubious journey, I keep asking myself, am I getting this right?...only to find that, after my father spent all that money on my elaborate education, the most basic history was inaccurately taught! It seems, we are going to have to revise all our history books.

My companions on this walk are educated people. They teach me that when Columbus did his "discovering," there were some 70 million inhabitants in the Americas; one hundred years later, in the name of crown, civilization, church, and progress, these numbers had been reduced by 90 percent, through massacre, through diseases brought by the new settlers, and by hunger following the killing of the buffalo.

Between 1503 and 1660, one hundred eighty-five tons of gold and ten thousand tons of silver were extracted from that lovely, vulnerable earth and sent back to prop up the failing economies of Europe. The Arawak Indians were forced to mine this treasure-trove. So brutal was their treatment, that by 1640 not a single Arawak remained on the island where Columbus landed. Before the annihilation, 1,000 indigenous people were sent back to Spain as slaves. Of course, the "Indians" of the Americas were not all one people, any more than the Europeans were. Some Native Americans survived the onslaught, in various tribes and locations. How did the descendants of such stalwarts make out, down the years? Strategists suggest that except for distinguished individuals, they are the poorest of the poor, poorest in health, poorest in life expectancy, poorest in housing, lowest in income and highest in unemployment, in 1991.

Who wants to celebrate Columbus Day? Not many people I know. To preserve a holiday, the name may be changed to Indigenous Peoples' Day. Paula Gunn Allen, in her marvelous book, *The Sacred Hoop*, perceives a Native American Renaissance. She teaches the reader about a matriarchal and matrifocal culture that had been flourishing in the Americas prior to the arrival of the men in ships. She suggests that it was not "the savages" but rather the positions of leadership assigned to women that most alarmed the conquest-minded. European men feared to erode their own authority by making treaties with women leaders, and made every effort to remove women from positions of authority. All records pertaining to a gynocratic social order among American Indians prior to 1,800 were destroyed. In 1992, Paula Gunn Allen urges people to celebrate, not <u>discovery</u> but <u>survival</u>, "...our amazing ability to endure, recover and restore our Native values and life ways, and blossom."

The native people could not have guessed at the numbers of white men intruding on their living space, but they could see it happening where they stood. We can console ourselves that we were not yet born, but now each of us - Indian or Anglo (a name the native people where I live use to include all interlopers), must meet this history in our own time and awareness, and do something or not do something about it. In California, the story is not long gone. Living elders in my area remember when white men "hunted" Indians on horseback.

Who were these people? Our precursors were hunters, fisherpeople, doctors, gamblers, currency makers, who walked many miles to the Pacific Ocean to gather clam shells, from which money was made. The Pomo basketry is considered so fine that it is exhibited at the Smithsonian Institute. Native artisan, Elsie Allen, was invited to Washington to show how the intricate designs were woven with wild colorings and sedge. The Pomos' was a family culture; without family one was nothing. Way down in history, I am filled with remorse for injuries endured the South Valley triblet of the Central Pomo. California's first constitution denied citizenship to the very men and women who were here first...by thousands of years! What strange assumptions were applied to the amenable language of "homesteading". *The Indians were at home.*

I wonder if suffering clings to the land. I try to transmute features I see around me, into the faces of the past. Handsome people, darker than my family, brown skin harmonizing with nature. I still my clattering typewriter to speak their names. I explore the meaning of my temptation to print that which has not been given to me. Do I even know their true names, the names a mother living among invaders whispers to a child? I found myself raging at little things: when Russell and I first came to Mendocino County, Indians were not supposed to try on clothes at the dress shop; Indians were supposed to sit in the balcony of a movie house, now long gone. Indians lived in weathered houses, unpainted. Eminent Native historian, Edna Guerrero, reminisced at PTA; her grandsons came to play with my children at "our" ranch; their mother seemed to like to talk with me at our long table, but she never asked me back. Hurt feelings were inappropriate, but what sort of feelings would fit better? I loved the boys' laughing eyes and coal black hair. I honor our Native American delegate to the Green Party, Margene McGee, and changed my registration to vote for her.

Indian friends tell me here, it's not all over; certain tribes are getting their land back. I must say, it does feel extremely immediate - and ancient, too - when a handful of folks, including a candidate for Congress, walk along a dusty road by way of saying "No" to the Board of Supervisors about to allow an asphalt batch plant to be built on the very border of the Reservation where it will help pave the highways we all use, but shorten the breath of an Indian elder, of an asthmatic child, and of anyone else who has time to notice the absence of pure air - in 1991. The press has been invited to come take a picture of our "march." They will. The Ukiah Daily Journal readers will see it in newsprint, look for faces they know, and wonder, "What that's all about?" Why do we do such little acts of principle? Holly says she cannot think of any other way she would choose to live. I like to quote my children.

Sitting on a wooden bench in a little public park, I watch who comes and goes in this grassy, urban space. A few students from the "continuation school" - a program for teenagers who are

126

not "making it," a stylistically colorful group, less "dumb" than defiant - sit on the grass and smoke. Lounging here is not a real *classy* thing to do, so I tell myself that in regard to my dubious journey, I have arrived - or perhaps my travels have simply been shunted to the lanes of my mind. I think, but what I think about has little to do with *class*.

Leo Banks, of Tucson, tells of a silver-haired Fulbright scholar who wants to plant 80 redwood trees in Galicia, Spain within view of where the Santa Maria was built - <u>New World trees on Old World soil</u>.

Noel Brown, with the United Nations Environmental Program, sees our times as "a moment in history when a new ecological alliance in the service of the earth is possible...as we redefine security no longer in military terms." He suggests "modifying a country's debt in exchange for a reforestation program." Now, there is a creative sense of the commensurate! I would love to vote for that at the polling place! Youngsters taking part in workshops at the University of Colorado at Boulder identify our problems. They call on themselves to <u>recycle, preserve, conserve, restore</u>. Miya Yoshitani, a reporter from the Christian Science Monitor, sends back word of a significant pronouncement from their conference in Boulder. "For too long the environmental movement was seen as a white, middle-aged movement. We want a broad-based movement, a grassroots movement. We have a very strong involvement by people of color." That's better!

Will the children of today find ways to welcome homeless people and recognize their diversity was the promise of the Statue of Liberty?

I watch my little grandsons honing their skills in unremitting battle, and hope that they, too, will have the chance to enlist in such worthy causes, jousting in defense of the *semper virens* redwoods, the habitat of owls, the diversity of plants and animal life. Does that include fish? Fish are in! We go to great lengths around here to relaunch a beached whale, or save a bag, or devise a less wasteful packaging that is less dependent on oil or less hard on trees. "Plastic or paper?" the grocery clerk asks. "Neither. I brought my own sack."

Holly and Ronnie Gilbert, who I first heard with the Weavers, performed at the Sisterfire Womens Music Festival in Washington, DC.

On the road with Holly, her road manager, Mary Bugnon, and her pianist, John Bucchino - this event celebrated feminism in the 90s.

CHAPTER FIFTEEN

Discovering "Women"

In my dubious journey, I discovered Columbus. I also discovered "women!" I have to acknowledge that I had never thought to ask <u>woman questions</u> until the surfacing of the women's movement. For example, I had never asked myself whether the individual woman, grandly standing in for the collective concept, had really wanted to have her baby in the shade of a Conestoga wagon on the open prairie, or whether she would have as lief stayed home with her mother and her friends in Lancaster where the wagon was purchased...instead of riding along with a husband as he fled *his* political persecution, *his* financial failure, the tedium of *his* work for someone else. What a rough journey she had, balancing on that high, wooden bench, although a lot less chancy than facing life without her man - perhaps the one her father chose for her. I had never thought that way about women pioneers.

Many of the teachers I studied with at Bennington College were women. I read Russian literature with Ursula Rossman, and the German Romantics with Eva Wunderlich, both refugees in 1938, a fact more impressive to me than gender. It is odd that, attending an all-woman college, I did not think about "women." Perhaps, burdened to know the high cost of my education, I was unconsciously trying to prove that my mind was as worthy of investment as my brother's...or, at least, no different from my brother's. In work for my college thesis - a comparative study of French, German, and English romanticism - I had read a lot of women writers. I thought of them as individuals - extraordinary persons such as Elizabeth Bronte or, in America, Emily Dickinson who would never have been put in a gender category, even one encompassing half the world. They were writers. And when I went looking for a job in 1941, women were welcome as men. It was wartime, everybody was hired; F for female. Fine. Of course, it wartime, everybody was hired; F for female. Fine. Of course, it was assumed that women would be glad to drop out when the soldiers came home.

But years later, when I lived in Ukiah, a professor started a group for women writers; we met in her home. She developed a course about women writers and offered to present it at Mendocino College. "Women Writers? Great! And shall the school offer a course called Men Writers?" she was ridiculed. Annette Parks, a Ph.D. now, is off and away teaching at the University of Wisconsin in the fields of cross cultural and ethnic studies. She has prevailed. *Women Writers* is now in the curriculum of Mendocino College. But how many women around the world have and must continue to demand gender consciousness? I go back and reread Virginia Woolf's *A Room of One's Own* as she articulates how men's institutions obstruct women's creativity. How sad it is that these men do not realize that our diminishment is their loss! Still, women will write and sing anyway, as women have done for centuries.

It was in the '70s in California that a matchless series of concerts called "Women-on-Wheels" brought forth an unprecedented audience, delirious with gratitude as it discovered itself, openly joyful as if after a long confinement veiled in secrecy. The performing musicians were Margie Adam, Cris Williamson, Meg Christian, and Holly Near. It was an historical event and although these women were not the first, nor the last, to sing what they called "women's music," it was an enormous introduction of feminist and lesbian song to an audience that had not been part of the inner circle. Even the mainstream press glowingly reviewed the tour as it traveled to seven California cities and one women's prison, taking the music to women who were not free to come. Ah, Sappho!

Russell and I attended the Women-on-Wheels concerts that came close to home. I could not have put into words what I learned that night, but as Holly writes it, "... we invited women to discover their lives apart from men, to blossom in self-esteem....even for those who do not actively lead lesbian lives, understanding the desire to love or make love to a woman is divine approval for making love to ourselves."

130

Why does my love make you
                shift in your chair
It's the bombs across the border that should
                make you tear your hair
And yet it's my love leaves you screaming out
                your nightmare
Perhaps there's something you know
                you should fear
If my love makes me strong
                and makes you disappear
It's simply love, my love for a woman

                from a song by Holly Near

Russell said he understood women loving women. "I love them, myself." He was such a mellow character!

I thought about this. I had gone to an all-girl grammar school and to a women's college, but it had never occurred to me to love anyone there - even my twin, even my closest friends, even my teachers - in the way women seemed to be loving each other at these concerts. And I could not play the disapproving heterosexual matron; the spirit was so generous and open and enthusiastic and affectionate...and there were so many people crowded into these halls! In the excitement, someone dropped a tape recorder from the balcony, but it didn't land on anyone. Good augury.

This explosion of feminist culture that emerged throughout the '70s and '80s filled my life and mind as well as that of my children. Timothy introduced American Sign Language to feminists attending *women's music* concerts and later, joined by dozens of interpreters and deaf activists, brought feminism to the hearing impaired. Laurel and Krissy's work with the Wallflower Order Dance Collective opened new vistas for women in dance...acknowledging the beauty in all body types, using natural movements from a variety of disciplines, taking each other's weight, they danced without a man on stage to hold them up. My son, Fred, is one of today's men who admires the strength and independence of women and tells his construction work crew that if they whistle at the women passing by, they will lose their jobs...in a manner of speaking.

Feminism, and particularly lesbian feminism, is not always easy to understand, for women or for men. Some "women's music" concerts were for women only...not expressly to be exclusive, but to create a cultural space as familiar as music itself, where women could feel completely free to be women apart from men. By law, at any auditorium of a school supported by public funds, no restrictions could be put on admission. Often, negotiations took place. Finally, permission for a woman only concert would be granted if it followed an open concert. Once Russell and I attended such an event. After the first show, we talked in the parking lot. "You go again, if you want to...might learn something. I'll just have a smoke." Waiting for me must have taken quite a few pipefuls! Russell was not defensive or afraid of other people's journeys, and our record collection includes songs by feminists, even outspoken lesbian songs I often heard him humming on his way to the barn. "...*Rugged women gone before me, paving paths like pioneers so off and all alone. I dreamed of queens and Cinderellas, but facing disappointment when I was grown.*"

Years later - it was some time after Russell had died - I became friends with the director of Rural Women's Resources, a local organization founded to support women. Rebecca Sandridge was the daughter of a piano teacher and a laborer - a union man - in the rubber industry in Akron, Ohio. Unlike either of her parents', her skin was slightly dark; she was proud of this evidence of blackness which she attributed to a male forbear who had presumed to visit the slave quarters. Wearing this fragment of history, and with her path illuminated by feminism, Rebecca felt a bond with women who had suffered the most cruel oppression, and was pledged to work for women's liberation, an all-inclusive banner held aloft.

It was great fun to be friends with Rebecca. Friendship is quite elegant when two people toss away notions of unrequited love in order to extend the parameters of being political allies. We also became tourists. We planned itineraries, inviting scenic places to be background for our talk. We did some Pacific wave watching and bistro sampling and redwood tree worshipping for which bona fide tourists fly three thousand miles. There was one problem I had not wanted to think about in spending so much time with a lesbian; her meanderings with me, so many years her senior, precluded ways she might have needed for herself. However that might have been, it was I who decided that I could not give so much time to friendship. I needed to be more alone if I was to be a writer, or even enter the depths of writer-consciousness. I blurted this out when Rebecca was at the wheel and navigating the hazardous mountain road from Fort Bragg to Willits. My timing was hideous. It was as if I was purposely declaring my decision while Rebecca was preoccupied with dangerous maneuvers. Rebecca had given up a lot for a unique experience: me. I expect she felt abandoned without notice, but she spoke no angry words to go on ringing down the years.

We did not see each very often after that day, but we wave at a distance - from Ukiah to Akron, where she returned to be home for her mother's final years. Occasionally we sent each other x-tras! Recently Rebecca sent an article she had written about the Iowa City National Conference on Racism, pleading with "white" women to start listening to the theories, visions, agendas, and leadership themes of women of color. "When 2 out of 3 adults are women, and 70% of the world's population are people of color, isn't it time," Rebecca asks, "that we lay down our hand-mirrors?" I miss Rebecca. She has class. Through her, I learned that I could proceed on my dubious journey more easily in the company of women. Women have participated in class, and suffered from it, and climbed the ladder on it, but they did not invent it. It's not of their doing. I have come to believe that women have priorities fundamentally different from men. Not all men. Exclude artists. And Saviours.

Appalled as I am by rumors of great suffering in our land, largely consigned to invisibility by obedient news editors reluctant to undermine the national psyche, I am proud to have found my way to many kindred souls who recognize a flaw in western civilization, truly a spiritual flaw at the very core of our vaunted know-how. Our American odyssey expresses a peculiar form of ambition uniquely tailored by the apparently endless expanse of "unused" land our forefathers failed to identify as a mirage. People lived there and it was not endless! We still pay for our blunder.

My daily newspaper reported that we had, at last, waged *a successful war*, short enough to be invigorating and with few casualties...although 170,000 Iraqi children are expected to die within a year or so as a result of that war. How dare one hand pretend not to see what the other hand has done! Our leaders send planeloads of medicine, but do not seem to comprehend the consequence of bombing what is called infrastructure: read people and the tasks they put together. I hear that it will take $30 billion to rebuild that society...if indeed that is even possible. Has my *dubious journey* taken me any further from the complicity of the upper classes? Not a whit. I was brought up on a sweet injunction. *Father, forgive them, for they know not what they do.* What then, Father, when we and they do know what we and they do? The culpability of *class* hovers over every issue.

Occasionally I get the feeling of being found out, unmasked, as in a play. I meet someone who recognizes...something. It's not just accent, but that's a symptom. I have noticed that my accent becomes stronger when I am nervous. I revert. I say I am a New Yorker, but I do not talk like a New Yorker from Brooklyn or the Bronx, with that worldly sound memorialized by taxi drivers on the TV screen. I do not explain. It's better to be a little odd, which indeed I am, and let it go at that. Nowadays, my hands are rough. I do my own work when I can and, for the rest, live companionably with it, undone. The roof is flaky; the sink is chipped; the attic is unapproachable. My life feels like it did in the Adirondacks when no servants were along...just us, just the family, and the evergreen spruce and the blue, blue water of the lake brooding above a leafy silt deeper down than I can dive. There is no one around to believe in *class* - certainly not the great grandchildren of those brave adventurers who found their first jobs in our households as "domestics." When they said, "Yessir! Yes Ma'am!", they were defending the distance between us because they could be summarily fired without cause. It continues to be hard to form a union for domestic workers, for "part-of-the-family!" Surely, household help did not think we were better than they. And I have spent my life learning that we were no worse. Ours was a polite or an emotionally repressed family in terms of behavior, but I know that "servants" were witness to some pretty bizarre goings-on. It was assumed they would not tell. Actually, they were treated as if they were not really there.

The war goes on in Ireland...Ruth and I felt the shadow of it when we traveled from Dublin to Belfast. We thought of Kate at every stile. Some newsbroker in America writes that Immigration and Naturalization Service is giving an unfair edge to people from Ireland. Still leaving home, Mavourneen?

On the West Coast, class partisans of the English language do not talk about *the wearin' of the green*. Rather, they deplore the evidence they see that California is turning into a "third world" state; they forget that Spanish was the language of the western coast, the language of the invaders that overwhelmed indigenous ways of talking and thus, eventually the language of the vanquished. Spanish is not new to California. We have a tragic border war, one on one, as refugees from poverty come north to find a job, and then go home to love and sleep. Desperate, some Mexican and Central American workers will travel as far as Kansas until they are caught and repatriated. They tell us, "Don't get the idea we want to live with you; we want to feed our kids!" The poor conditions in their homelands drive them to the very country that has participated in creating the poor conditions.

CHAPTER SIXTEEN

Central America with Holly

I have taken two journeys to Central America with my daughter, Holly. The first was to Nicaragua in 1984, where a revolutionary movement, brought forth by the Sandinistas, after having fought U.S.-backed forces since the 1930s, had at long last asserted itself as a very young government of *campesinos* and urban citizens. Huge land holdings (selfishly held out of production by nonresident owners, many of whom had second homes in Miami) were now distributed to be farmed by the Sandinistas. The excitement of the 50th Anniversary of Sandino, beloved patriot of the common people, was being celebrated at gigantic outdoor rallies where colorful banners were lifted in rhythm, and *consignas* chanted: *El pueblo unido jamas sera vencido!* and *Patria libre o murir!* I was there as Holly's mother-*madre* was a hallowed word - and Holly was guest of the FSLN: Frente Sandinista Liberacion Nacional.

In my own country I have, more often than not, been a painfully critical patriot; I have been so keenly aware of the unkept promises relative to our national credo. In Nicaragua, it was a new experience for me to attend huge rallies and small-town meetings in which participants were grasping so proudly the opportunities to which they were invited by their own government. The Sandinistas were dedicated to changing the indisputably cruel inequities of the Somoza era...which had, to our shame, been made possible by economic and military contributions from the USA. To Nicaraguan folks, in whom hope was awakening, Holly brought toys, school supplies, sound system components, musical instruments, film, as well as messages from Americans about whom the Nicaraguan people had no way of knowing. This redheaded young troubadour had credibility as she recalled what

136

she had been taught in public school about our own American Revolution. Empathy abounded!

Meetings and concerts had been set up in advance, with lots of room for spontaneous gatherings. Holly sang at a psychiatric hospital, a military training camp, a community center in a barrio, on television, and at the major cultural center in Managua. We also met with The Women's Union, The Mothers of Martyrs, workers from a clothing factory, educators, and many poets, writers, and musicians. How does one visit a revolution? Holly decided to go everywhere, see everything, and be of use whenever possible, even if we were tired. We adopted our Nicaraguan host's philosophy, "When building something new, like we are building a new life, one gets sleepy but never tired." After one neighborhood event, Holly, having heard that many attending had lost children in the war, sang her most outspoken peace songs. An old woman came up to me afterward, tears in her eyes, and although we did not share a verbal language or background, she extended her hand, rough from working the land...like mine. And we knew we shared a common outrage against war and a common ideal.

In 1992, with humility, I ponder the Nicaraguan people's vote against the FSLN, putting the U.S.-backed UNO Party in power. I imagine folks voted for food and a measure of tranquility, for if the Sandinistas were elected for a third term, the United States would continue to batter the revolutionary government as it struggled to deliver on its promises. It makes me sick to hear the Administration boast about largesse that was intended to come late, once the revolution had been made to fail. In the relief of the cease-fire, one wonders after all those years of war, how the wounds will be healed.

My second journey, in 1988, was to El Salvador. (I never tired of hearing that sonorous name as it was flung across the airwaves.) One day, Holly phoned home to say that she had been asked to attend *Un Canto Por La Paz*, an unprecedented festival of music to be held in that tragedy-laden country; she would be one of many musicians, mostly from the Southern Hemisphere, invited by the University of El Salvador and willing to go to a land that was sadly disreputable for its repression of its own people, for the killing of four American nuns, for invading its own university,

137

for the assassination of Archbishop Romero, for its death squads. "Mom, I think I'll go - what do you think?" Motherly, I was ambivalent but I conceded. "It would not be like you to refuse." An hour later I called back. "I think I'll go, too." "Good. I've already applied for both our visas."

"The festival was intentionally staged right out in the open, a week of concerts, workshops and gatherings. The coalition of organizers representing students, labor, human rights, women, and artists asked permission of the government. No answer was received, so they proceeded with the plans - posters and banners went up, stages were built, the available technology for sound pieced together. Elections were about to happen in El Salvador; for the benefit of the visiting press and witnesses, there would be a brief surcease of terror. It was into this breather that the astute Salvadorean cultural workers dreamed up *Un Canto Por La Paz*.

Holly and I arrived at the airport of San Salvador, formally reassuring as airports try to be - although one writer has referred to this one as a mausoleum. Our bags were searched and found to contain only clothes and pages of music. We had no trouble. Later, we learned that a friend flying in from Nicaragua had been questioned in an intimidating manner and warned not to take part in any demonstrations; May Day was right around the corner. We emerged into the new-feeling air of the Southern Hemisphere and a country known to harbor all the complexities of the geo-political world of the late 20th century. Holly and I said a sort of good-bye to each other in the sense that we would not indulge in the historical or political gossip that is creative among friends *learning live*. From now on, everything we said could be held against us - worse, maybe held against someone else.

There seemed to be no one to meet us among the well-dressed Salvadorans waiting for our plane. Perhaps our hosts did not want to draw attention by hanging around the airport much ahead of time. We waited. Then suddenly we were identified, welcomed by a young man we did not know, and taken up into a well-worn-in van which then bounded along the road to the city. I sat in the back with a woman from the university. Since, to my unending shame I did not speak her language, I admired the countryside and we smiled a lot. Our driver was a large fellow with a smooth face from which a hand seemed ever to try to erase

138

worry, and a smile one yearns to study again and again. He called himself Isaias Mata, a painter so talented that the galleries simply could not exclude him, even though they feared his work - which showed boldly painted images of men and women imprisoned, tortured, and undefeated by the dictators. Isaias says, "The people who can afford to buy my paintings do not. Perhaps they do not like them," he smiles. We learned that he is a key organizer of the festival and will be our *responsable*; like most political artists, he does many things besides making his art. I bought one of his paintings - only the second time in my life that I have bought an original work of art. The colors are those of wheat and blood and storm clouds. The picture shows a woman cradling a new baby. Her all-enveloping cloak extends beyond the canvas; her face is a human cry; there is a gun strapped to her back. She, who has just given birth, must defend this life with death! Four times a mother, four times a grandmother, I will take this picture to be framed, but I do not know how I will live with it. My worst fear is that I will get used to it!

We started out housed, for security, in a fairly expensive hotel. Holly moves calmly but with caution. I admire how she respects complexities and takes the safety of her hosts, as well as of herself and her traveling companions, seriously.

The first evening at the hotel we met an American who had lost both legs in Vietnam. He comes to El Salvador to find victims of a war that seems conscienceless to him. He measures those who have lost an arm, a leg. He goes back to the States and constructs the needed limb at the laboratory of his university rehab center. The veteran returns to say to a child in El Salvador, "Walk!"

On our second day, we were driven by jeep along a dusty road to a rural parish where a North American minister has found her calling. A lusty choir practice is in full swing. Many friendly hands help us find our place in the hymnal. One tune is *Mine Eyes Have Seen The Glory* and another is Bob Dylan's *Blowin' In The Wind* - both melodies carry Salvadoran words.

We visited a Christian Base Community where many young people take turns reading the scriptures aloud. John 10, 11-18, Apostles 4, 8-13, John 3, 1-2. A North American *padre* serves Communion and urges his parishioners to be *buen' pastores*. He speaks of the courage it takes to work on the side of the people. "Look to The Shepherd, and at other times, become the shepherd. Listen to the sounds beyond your flock. *Campesinos, campesinas,* direct your thoughts to your family, your community, and also to your world!"

As Holly moved along her path in the complex role of a peaceable North American in El Salvador, attentive without fail, responding where she could, I looked at my child, nurtured in the rural community of Potter Valley which took time to enjoy its children. It was there that she received the grounding from which to start on the road from Hollywood to Hiroshima, from a feminist conference in North Dakota to a rape crisis center in Arkansas, from the land of the aborigines in Australia to a new revolution in Nicaragua, from a Women's International League for Peace and Freedom (WILPF) meeting in Belgium to an atomic test site protest in Nevada, to a gay and lesbian march in San Francisco, to a peace march with her father in Washington, D.C.- again and again - and to El Salvador. Holly wrote later, "There is renewed energy in my country for creative protest...huge demonstrations against arms shipments to Central America, gigantic concern for the AIDS crisis, opposition to sending our boys across the seas to fight. Music plays an essential part. This is what I do."

Back at our hotel in San Salvador, an interview was set up for Holly. We sat around a table out on a patio. The ever present Coca Cola was served. Off to one side sat the also ever present government agent who listened in on the interview. His arrogance filled the room, and he felt no need to disguise himself. Holly spoke diplomatically and like a poet - not saying and saying.

On Sunday we visited a prison. We stood among families holding baskets of food and kerchiefs full of necessities. The guards took our passports; after Holly explained that we'd come to visit a friend, they allowed us to enter with the other visitors. We followed the crowd along lanes between low buildings until we came to a broad dirt area with a few benches. Most of the women here had been incarcerated for alleged stealing or prostitution. I ponder these crimes in a country where fields have been planted to export crops while the people have no land on which to grow their food. We are told that even the poor farmers must buy instant coffee! A parable.

The woman Holly came to visit was a political prisoner. She told her story eloquently. She had been accused of selling eggs at the air force base so that she could spy for the guerrillas, the FMLN (Farabundo Marti Liberacion Nacional). I was surprised to learn that she believed she owed her life to the letter writing efforts of people in the USA; such campaigns force the government to take cases seriously - *if this person is harmed, there will be trouble up the line*. And then I wondered, who are these elite people from d'Aubisson's Arena Party who demand so much death to secure their lives? It is almost impossible for someone who was once a child roller skating on Park Avenue to get it straight, but I try to reach down through my inherited assumptions of us as kindly people to grasp the agonizing themes we need to drum into our heads.

As Holly became more acclimated, she moved our group of four (pianist, translator, mother, and self) to a small downtown hotel where the other musicians who had come from throughout The Americas were staying. The hotel, worn and clean, was close to the civic plaza where the final concert would take place. A single plate meal of rice and beans and lettuce was served at any time the individual artists could get home to eat; the coffee, ah, this was where coffee comes from!

The person who was Holly's original contact in the States greeted the musicians in an orientation meeting. Tall, slender, soft-spoken, not reckless, he provides statistics that are unimaginable to us: lives lost, refugees, hunger never fully assuaged, unemployment. Later, driving around, we notice that in spite of all the "aid" from the United States, the government has not repaired the earthquake damage - at least, not in the barrios. I wonder about this, because I know the generosity with which American people responded to news of this particular natural disaster. We find documented information that much of this outpouring of USA sympathy lined the pockets of the Salvadoran rich, trained counterinsurgency troops, bought military equipment, made war on a people whose needs are so like ours: food, shelter, learning, forming unions, bargaining collectively, being secure against police attack, not being abducted, not being followed by unmarked cars, not being *disappeared*.

The musicians were divided into two groups for the travels outside of San Salvador. One group went to Santa Ana, one to San Miguel. We all would meet back in San Salvador for a cultural forum, a concert at the university and for the final open air concert at the Plaza.

Singers know hundreds of songs. They couple words with melodies like a painter prepares a palette. The progression of songs through an evening with an audience represents a series of choices that are not accidental; often I have seen Holly change her set list midstream. When she phones me - from London or Missoula, Amherst or Saigon - my second question always is, "What did you sing?" And so similarly I wondered in El Salvador, where beneath the winter sun the heart well knows the dirge. Talking with her host, Holly asked, "Should I be careful?" He answered, "Not you. The danger is ours. Be discreet until the festival begins, then sing whatever you wish. The Salvadoran artists will express more than you can think." He knew that everyone participating in any large or small capacity, including the hotel staff who were willing to welcome us, put his or her life on the line. Some of the organizers were extremely visible, appearing with Holly at the radio station, everywhere.

And so I waited to learn what Holly would sing. During one of our walks through the market, she thought out-loud, "should I sing songs in English, outspoken political songs from the United States, so that they will know there is a progressive force in my country that supports their independence and their desire for peace? Or should I sing in Spanish, songs written by great Latin American composers, that reflect universal dreams but detail more specifically Latin American experience?" She chose three songs in Spanish, *Te Doy Una Cancion, Gracias a la Vida* and *Llamada Encendida* - familiar to most of the audience - and her own *Hay Una Mujer Desaparecida,* which was listened to in hushed affirmation; every family in that audience knew someone who had been disappeared. As much as I might have wanted Salvadorans to know of our radical traditions, it became clear throughout our visit that the most radical thing North Americans can do is listen.

142

It meant a great deal to people that Holly knew their songs...and that her mother would also make the journey to their country.

Amparo Ochoa, a striking woman from Mexico, seemed to put her arms around every audience. Her songs, often about the work and struggles of the campesinos, moved people to their feet cheering a single phrase of revolutionary song. Through her person, I could comprehend that all the artists were chosen for their way in the world. She delighted the children and brought a few on stage to sing with her, unrehearsed; she also threw back a paper airplane that landed on her head as she sat in the audience. Another singer from the United States was fascinating to the Salvadoran children through her beaded dreadlocks and African clothes. There were musicians from Venezuela, Costa Rica, Brazil, Argentina, Mexico, the USA, and of course, El Salvador. I see their faces as I think their names, many showing Indian roots, sons and daughters of colonists and indigenous peoples, making music together.

Holly took part in forums about the *nueva cancion* at the University of El Salvador campuses. In 1980, tanks and armored cars and soldiers had fired into classrooms, killing teachers and students. The university was closed. There was no longer an institution of higher learning in El Salvador, a devastating void for the country's future artists, scientists, intellectuals, technicians, doctors, lawyers and economists. And, as it had intended to do, the military destroyed the legitimate meeting place of popular organizations who coordinated initiatives for change. Four years later, with incredible sacrifice on the part of students, teachers, administrators and janitors, the university doors were reopened, but without government support, and only as a result of intense pressure from abroad. It was in a building at the university that we came across a concrete floor strewn with banners being hand-lettered to be hung across the street. There were yards of paper and tubs of paint in every color.

UN CANTO POR LA PAZ
SOBERANIA Y INDEPENDENCIA
EN EL SALVADOR

143

(Vividly I recalled Jeff Langley and Holly crouching on the grass in Doolan Canyon, Ukiah, as they painted banners that would fly across Main Street USA, announcing their concert.) Back then, they sang songs of love and mourned the war against Vietnam.

In El Salvador, as if for the first time, I heard Holly speak about our North American history. She spoke of the struggles from which our distinctly North American music arises, of the indigenous peoples, of the religious communities fleeing persecution in Europe, of the immigrants escaping economic oppression, of the sweatshops endured by workers until they formed industrywide unions, of the Africans in slavery and how they achieved their freedom, and must go on achieving their freedom. She spoke of the poor, of women.

Salvadoran audiences, who enjoy clapping to a beat, adopted *Oh Mary, Don't You Weep, Don't You Mourn*, and when Holly's accompanist, Barbara Higbie, mixing in strands of American culture, played a fiddle-hoe-down before the closing verse of the spiritual, it brought the house down, out there on the concrete bleachers of a soccer field, one evening beneath a rosy moon in El Salvador. *Otra! Otra!*

To be invited to sing by the opposition in a war-torn country is not quite the same as being invited to sing at Zellerbach Hall in Berkeley. A different history intrudes upon the ambiance of the event. Holly carried with her a letter to the U.S. ambassador, appreciating whatever courtesy he might extend, and inviting him to attend any part of this history-making expression of democracy. If he did come, he did not make himself known; he did not appear on the platform to encourage the artists for peace assembled there from many countries including his own.

The grand finale was to be an open concert in the plaza of San Salvador, a sun-drenched square framed on one side by the unfinished Cathedral where Father Romero was murdered by the right-wing forces who feared his criticism of their torture and brutality, and on the other side, the government buildings that had survived the earthquake. All of the musicians would perform, including a "surprise performance" by a group that had been banned from El Salvador. Without concern for permission, the people by the thousands poured into the plaza from center city, the suburbs, the countryside. They simply occupied the space. The Government and the Army circled but on this day they did not intervene - no embarrassing word would get back to the U.S. Congress that a recipient of a large "grant-in-aid" claiming to promote and protect democracy would not permit a music festival. The festival organizers had known this would be true and took advantage of the window of opportunity, aware that the dangers would surface later.

We had met earlier in the day with artists who said, "When you go, don't forget about us. If the government forces come for us, make sure they know you know." The artists laid out a plan that Holly would follow if and when this happened. Then they sat quietly with each other. There was nothing more to say. It was time now for the music.

Throughout my life I have found that such enormous exhilaration, as I was feeling, is painfully tempered by a following downbeat. I try to prepare for it; it can't be done. Here is a case in point.

Holly was introduced early in the concert because she had to leave to meet a previously scheduled commitment to a support-network for women in prison...in St. Louis! She sang, then after saying farewell, she once again rode the little festival van to the airport; it was driven by last-minute enlisted *companeros* who were anxious to be off the road by dark. I traveled along with her to say good-bye, then returned to experience the rest of the festival and the demonstration that would take place the following day. May Day.

In the meantime, Holly's plane was reported late, and late again, and late again. The airport cleared of all travelers except for those on her flight. She watched the government police pace back and forth with their guns. Holly would wait for five lonely hours that she could have spent with other artists at the festival. If the plane did not come, she would not call the festival organizers to risk their safety on the dark roads to come and get her, and she knew there was great risk for a woman to take a cab alone at night along that highway. In solitary companionship with her notebook she wrote, "I let my mind imagine for a moment the details of my fear; this is what Salvadorans live with every day, helplessness in a chaotic dictatorship, mis-information, never

145

knowing..." Holly found personal and political meaning in her experience that night. But for my part, I shall never recover from the decision - for whatever reasons - to leave my child, compatriot and friend alone at the airport in El Salvador. All that I can say is that I have disappointed myself more than life has ever disappointed me.

Actually, all turned out fine. The plane did at last arrive; Holly's trip continued to be hard, (flat tires on the airplane, airport curfews in Mexico) but she reached the stage door in St. Louis ten minutes before curtain time. The festival in El Salvador was brought to a close without government interference - exuberantly, exhaustedly, victoriously.

The next day, although the city was full with people who had attended the festival, thousands more arrived in the dawn to participate in a May Day demonstration. The banners protested the government and called for a fair and peaceful election. Many faces were covered with red and black bandanas to avoid being photographed by the death squads.

As I took part in May Day in El Salvador, which celebrated spring with a huge gathering of working people arriving on foot from the far reaches of the countryside - a major commitment for them to leave their fields unattended - I tried to evoke May Day in my own country. On the ranch, the children presented me with a crown of wild flowers. On occasion I had visited Ruth to watch the dancing children weave the ribbons round the maypole, but I knew there was more; I had to look up the Haymarket riot.

A People and a Nation told the history I was seeking:

> ...in the late 1800s, a number of labor groups, including the Knights of Labor, began to campaign for an eight-hour work day. This effort...gathered most momentum in Chicago, where radical anarchists, as well as various craft unions - perhaps as many as 100,000 workers in all - agitated for the cause. On May 1, 1886, the workers' deadline for achieving their goal, city police were mobilized to prevent possible disorder,

146

especially among striking workers at the huge McCormick reaper factory. The day passed calmly, but two days later, police stormed an area near the McCormick plant, and broke up a battle between striking unionists and non-union workers hired as strike-breakers. Police shot and killed two unionists and wounded several others. The next evening, labor groups organized a rally at Haymarket Square, near downtown Chicago, to protest police brutality. As a company of police officers approached the meeting, a bomb exploded near their front ranks, killing seven and injuring sixty-seven. Mass arrests of anarchists and unionists followed. Eventually, eight men, all anarchists, were tried and convicted of the bombing, though there was no evidence of their guilt. Four were executed and one committed suicide in prison. The remaining three were pardoned in 1893 by Illinois governor John P. Altgeld, who believed they had been victims of the "malicious ferocity" of the courts. The Haymarket riot drew public attention to labor campaigns for better conditions, but also revived middle-class fear of radicalism...

The newly formed American Federation of Labor was the major workers' organization to emerge after the 1863 upheavals. May 1st is celebrated all over the world as an international workers' day. Ironically, it is virtually unknown in the United States and is often thought to be a holiday invented by some communist country. Here in El Salvador it is a day of hope.

CHAPTER SEVENTEEN

A Dubious Journey

When Ruth died of cancer in the spring of 1991 - she who had used her body so well, as wife and mother of six children, as teacher, skier, dancer, walker, artist, early childhood education consultant, infant care giver, twin - it was an eclectic group of mourners who gathered for a service at the Unitarian Church which was so much a path into her city experience of Philadelphia.

First Unitarian Church of Philadelphia
April Forum: April 12, 1992
❧
When is Daddy Coming Home? Parenting on Both Sides of the Prison Bars
❧
Remembering Ruth Bacon: Vince Whitney, Chair, First Unitarian Church
Social Concerns Committee
❧
Forum Panelists:
Marnie Henretig: Advocate with Pennsylvania Prison Society
Lufay Butler: Coordinator of Prisoner and Family Services at Episcopal Family Service
Barbara Pressman: Volunteer at Graterford Prison
Joan Gauker: Volunteer Coordinator at Graterford Prison
Delica (Nissa) Sulaiman: Family Member of Graterford Prisoner
Justine Reyes: Mother of a Muncie Inmate
Rev. Judy Buck-Glenn: Moderator
❧
Ruth Holmes Bacon (May 5, 1916-May 10, 1991) was a long-time member of First Unitarian Church and an active advocate for many causes. One of the greatest of her concerns was for prisoners and their families, especially their children.
❧
This forum is dedicated to her memory and her work.
❧
"For I was in prison and you visited me..."

A black man rose to speak of Ruth Bacon's work at Graterford maximum security prison. Was he, himself, a prisoner on extraordinary leave in Ruth's honor? "She was a friend to these men," he said.

As her twin, I felt I should be a presence, and yet wondered if my resemblance to Ruth would sadden her friends or even startle those who did not know she had a twin; in her neighborhood I have often been greeted familiarly with her name. I tried to think of something I could say without a quivering voice and devastated mien that Ruth would have found embarrassing in public conduct; it is hard - and shameful - to be trying to think of something to say while others are speaking from the soul. Into a moment of silence, I cast these words. "Living from the day of our birth in such proximity, we early on knew that we dare not be rivals; there was nothing to do but be the best of friends - a parable for the sort of world Ruth believed in." The choir began the only hymn, quite unplanned, which was their gift to Ruth.

I miss Ruth in a way I had not fully anticipated, since it has been years since we had lived together, but Ruth was the one I called, Potter Valley to Philadelphia, to ask, "Can you believe...Aren't you amazed?...Can you imagine?...What do you think?" She was my mind's companion, more so than my husband, more than my children. All are strangers compared with Ruth because they are the biggest part of the happiness and stress we talked about together. We both believed as we had been taught at the Madison Avenue Presbyterian Church - and had already learned between ourselves - that *blessed are the peacemakers*. I do not know an incontrovertible meaning of peace, to which all can subscribe. It is a huge word that has nothing to do with apathy or tolerance of injustice or nonmilitary sanctions which, to choose a current example, limit Iraq's ability to restore its electrical system, its sewer, its system for providing uncontaminated water, for importing food and medicine, for picking up its life.

Ruth and I were friends. Friends are kept or lost, day by day, deed by deed, a phone call made or missed, a resource shared or hoarded, a treaty kept or broken. To borrow Holly's words, *friendship is paying attention*, person to person or worldwide. But to raise our voices in the world requires the

149

practice of intelligent inquiry and courage to accept the consequences of what we decide to believe, whether we are right or wrong. The peace of silence in our times is not blessed. The peace we speak of is the peace that passeth all understanding, virtually unimaginable in a world rife with conflict everywhere, its details hard to understand. The peace we aspire to is a global activist peace. Human beings know about each other now, world around, because of the unprecedented communications technology that brings a village meeting in Somalia into the living room of a city council member in Ukiah. Terrifyingly, it is this same level of technology that could destroy the whole planet.

Of course, I did not see all this when, as a child, with Ruth squeezing in beside me, I climbed up on the radiator, early morning, before the janitor sent up the hot steam, and peered out the narrow bathroom window - west to the gray dawn over Central Park, east to the sunrise bursting over tenements beyond Lexington Avenue to the East River. One can see very little of New York City from Park Avenue and Seventy-second Street, but I did sense that something was wrong with me, some unseemly privilege through which a salutary contact with common people - the camaraderie of ragamuffins - had been forfeited. This childhood wisdom became the lodestar guiding me beyond my parents' horizon, to a cabin high on a hill in North Pownal, Vermont, to the three R's on Broadway interpreted for actors under twelve, to a birthing clinic in Hazard County, Kentucky, to a hospitality house on Mott Street in the Bowery, to a vacation for city kids on a farm in Pennsylvania, to the Boulevard Raspail in Paris and an old taco on the road to Quimper in Brittany, to a radical school in Arkansas and a radical theater in Philadelphia, to an airplane hanger in Los Angeles, and a toy shop in Montrose using war surplus parts, to a cattle ranch in Potter Valley and a sheep ranch in Hopland, to Nicaragua and to El Salvador, diametrically opposite fiefs where Holly sang to people of like mind, to Indian reservations in Taos and in Pinoleville, near home (Yokayo, which Northern Europeans mispronounced as Ukiah, is the Pomo name for deep valley), to a place of friendship on the island of Key West, to that country in the mind where my twin once lived, to the places endeared to me as background of my children's lives, and to my home on Clay Street, named after a president who included instructions in his Will that all freed slaves be taught reading, writing and arithmetic, and then shipped back to Africa.

In August of 1992, a touring Chautauqua company set up a large tent in Ukiah's public park with the sponsorship of various local cultural groups including the Ukiah Playhouse and the Humanities Department at Mendocino College. Some thousand citizens attended *Columbus and After, Rethinking The Legacy*, and took part in a sometimes passionate dialogue that followed between Native Americans, European immigrants, and an extraordinarily able moderator borrowed from a California university. Columbus, Father Junipero Serra, Jessie Benton Fremont, and Antonio Garra, leader of the Indian Tax Revolt of 1851, all appeared on stage to have their say; some ideas were hard to listen to. Later, removing their costumes, these historian/actors discussed the roles of the characters they had represented.

Sally Roesch Wagner played Jessie Fremont, the woman who had composed colorful reports to Washington, D.C., about her husband's exploits, thus firing the national imagination for westward ho! In an article in Akwe:Kon Journal, Wagner reports that Indian men were not unmindful of the inferior position of women in white culture, and that a Seneca chief urged that women be treated as well as they were in his nation. Sally Roesch Wagner writes, "While the western theory of feminism came from dissidents who were chastised by the church or arrested by the state for their ideas, the Iroquois practiced feminism. Suffragists believed that the idea of equality was uniquely indigenous to the Native people." I think the Indian speaker, Antonio Rivera, at the Ukiah Chautauqua, said all I need to know to finish my journey...until I came across a book by Paula Gunn Allen. I remember my dream of the Indian brave who advised me to drink of the waters of Lake Honnedaga, where I would learn all I needed to know. Dreams transform experience, but they are also limited by it. If I had read Paula Gunn Allen's *The Sacred Hoop*, my dream figure might have been a woman, and I would have been inspired by "...a culture which was dedicated to peace, balance, harmony and respect for all that is." There I wish to belong.

Finally, I turn back to my friend, Dorothy Andersen, who first started me wondering to this theme. She writes from Arizona

151

where she has gone with her husband, Alfred F. Andersen, author of *Liberating the Early American Dream*. Dorothy protests, "Why do you call your journey 'dubious'?" She sends me poetry from her dictionary, poetry of correlative meanings. <u>Dubious</u>: uncertain, equivocal, undetermined, characterized by qualities that occasion mistrust, of doubtful promise, ambiguous, skeptical, hanging in the balance...even shady! Thoughtfully, I couple each word with my journey and conclude that I named it well.

NOTES

I wish to acknowledge and thank the following authors, whose works served as valuable resources in writing this book.

Allen, Paula Gunn. *Sacred Hoop: Recovering the Feminine in American Indian Traditions.* Boston: Beacon Press, 1986.

Brown, Rita Mae. *Plain Brown Wrapper.* Baltimore: Diana Press, 1976.

Fowlie, Wallace. *Pantomime, A Journal of Rehearsals.* Chicago: H. Regnery Co., 1951.

Frost, Robert. *A Swinger of Birches.* Owings Mills, MD: Stemmer House, 1982.

Lindsay, Vachel. *The Congo & Other Poems.* New York: The MacMillan Co., 1922.

Maurin, Peter. *The Green Thumb Revolution.* New York: Sheed & Ward, 1936.

McPherson, James. *Marching Toward Freedom: the Negro Civil War 1861-1865.* New York: Knopf, 1968.

Norton, Mary Beth, David M. Katzman, Paul D. Escott, Howard P. Chudacoff and William M. Tuttle, Jr. *A People and A Nation: A History of the United States.* Boston: Houghton Mifflin Co., 1986.

Reynolds, Quentin. *The Fiction Factory.* New York: Random House, 1955.

Rounds, Stowell. *Men and Birds in South America.* Fort Bragg, CA: Q.E.D. Press, 1990.

Anne Holmes Near grew up on Park Avenue in the Depression years of the '30s, roller skated with her twin sister in New York's famous oasis, Central Park, played with horses in the fields of her parents' second home on Long Island, and was vaguely aware that the family wherewithal came from STREET & SMITH, publishers of *Love Story* and *Detective Story*, which their mother never read. These are the determining ingredients.

Chauffeur-driven for thirteen years to Miss Chapin's School for Girls, Ms. Near received that enviable education which inspires a student to want to learn and go on learning about the whole-wide-world. Four years at Bennington College helped with the specifics.

When World War II exposed the racism in Hitler's Germany, Anne Near, a life-long pacifist, took a train west and hired on at a factory making B-29s. When the atomic bomb was dropped on Hiroshima, the shocked family sought "good work", raising cows in Northern California - sixteen years of redemptive labor. When the Viet Nam War divided the heart of the country, Anne Near marched in peace demonstrations. From Park Avenue to a factory assembly line, from riding a bike in Salzburg, to riding a tractor in Hopland, this is the ambiguous story referred to in the title, *A DUBIOUS JOURNEY* From Class to Class.